DATE DUE

APR 1 – 1995	
APR 1 – 1995	
MAR 3 1 1995	
MAR 3 1 1995	
MAR 1 8 1996	
MAR 2 3 1996	
MAR 1 1 1996	
NOV 1 3 1998	
NOV 2 3 1998	
MAY – 6 2008	
APR 2 9 2008	

GAYLORD   PRINTED IN U.S.A.

STRESS AMONG OLDER ADULTS

ABOUT THE AUTHOR

James H. Humphrey, Professor Emeritus at the University of Maryland, has published over 60 books that have been adopted for use in over 1,200 institutions of higher learning in this country and abroad. Several of his most recent books have been in the area of stress. His 200 articles and research reports have been published in over 20 different national and international journals. A notable researcher in the area of stress education, he is the founder and editor of *Human Stress: Current Selected Research* published annually by AMS Press, Inc. In the early 1980s he collaborated with the late Hans Selye on certain aspects of stress research. Dr. Humphrey has received numerous educational honors and awards. He is a Fellow in the American Institute of Stress.

STRESS AMONG OLDER ADULTS
Understanding and Coping

By

JAMES H. HUMPHREY, Ed.D.

Professor Emeritus
University of Maryland

With a Foreword by
Paul J. Rosch, M.D.
President of the American Institute of Stress

CHARLES C THOMAS • PUBLISHER
Springfield • Illinois • U.S.A.

Published and Distributed Throughout the World by

CHARLES C THOMAS • PUBLISHER
2600 South First Street
Springfield, Illinois 62794-9265

© *1992 by* CHARLES C THOMAS • PUBLISHER

ISBN 0-398-05790-7

Library of Congress Catalog Card Number: 92-3366

With THOMAS BOOKS *careful attention is given to all details of manufacturing
and design. It is the Publisher's desire to present books that are satisfactory as to their
physical qualities and artistic possibilities and appropriate for their particular use.*
THOMAS BOOKS *will be true to those laws of quality that assure a good name
and good will.*

Printed in the United States of America
SC-R-3

Library of Congress Cataloging-in-Publication Data

Humphrey, James Harry, 1911–
    Stress among older adults : understanding and coping / by James H.
Humphrey ; with a foreword by Paul J. Rosch.
        p.   cm.
    Includes bibliographical references and index.
    ISBN 0-398-05790-7 (cloth)
    1. Stress in old age.   2. Stress management for the aged.
I. Title.
RA777.6.H865   1992
155.9′042′0846 — dc20
                                                    92-3366
                                                    CIP

FOREWORD

A variety of research confirms a significant increase in the prevalence of stress related complaints and disorders in older individuals. In many ways, certain aspects of Aging appear almost synonymous with chronic stress. In his later years, Hans Selye actually modified his original definition of stress in favor of "the rate of wear and tear on the body"—which is a pretty good definition of the aging process. Aging also appears to be equated with a declining ability to cope with stress. An old German colloquialism, which literally translates as "you are looking old," essentially implies that you are unable to cope with some stress related problem.

Although the term is freely used, Aging is actually a surprisingly difficult concept to nail down. The word obviously means growing older. However, our primary interest here is in *biologic* rather than *chronological* age. How should this be defined? More importantly, how can it be measured?

Several years ago, I presided over an International Symposium on Aging, conducted under the auspices of the Biotonus Clinic in Montreaux, Switzerland. Distinguished researchers from all over the world, including a Nobel laureate, attempted to grapple with this problem. It was clear that in humans, there are consistent anatomic and physiologic consequences of biologic aging, including osteoporosis and osteoarthritis. There are also specific disorders that are seen more frequently in the elderly, including maturity onset diabetes, emphysema, hypertension, Alzheimer's and Parkinson's diseases, keratotic skin lesions and certain malignancies. There are distinct characteristic signs of aging which can be demonstrated under the microscope, in the form of cellular changes in various tissues. There may be atrophy of some organs, hyperplasia and hypertrophy in others, or tell-tale pigments and staining characteristics in specific tissues and cells. There are also increased extracellular hallmarks, such as arteriosclerosis, amyloid and immune complex deposits, fractures, intervertebral disc degeneration, cataracts, pulmonary emboli, etc.

A variety of laboratory studies can be used to assess biologic aging, particularly certain immune system markers. Physiologic aging can be evaluated clinically by such things as hair graying scores, reduction in skin elasticity, hearing, visual acuity, vital capacity and vibration perception, as well as progressive changes in blood pressure, heart size, stature, hand grip strength and reaction time responses. All of the above can be considered to represent criteria for biologic aging. However, it is important to emphasize that each of these can also be influenced by many other factors not related to aging. Indeed, the panel concluded that the only consistency between any of these measures and aging—or with each other, *is their inconsistency.*

Despite the arguments and controversy about the significance and relative merit of these various parameters and benchmarks, there was a surprising unanimity of opinion about the important role of stress. Most of the participants agreed that stress could contribute to, or exaggerate, almost every facet of the aging process. It seemed equally clear that certain stress related problems in the elderly appear to be somewhat unique, and that appropriately designed stress reduction approaches could be efficacious in preventing some of these adverse health consequences, and also significantly improve the overall quality of life in the geriatric population.

As Dr. Humphrey points out in this valuable contribution to the subject, such problems and concerns are rapidly growing. The number of Americans over 65 has increased more than 14% since 1980, compared to an increase of only 5% for those under this age. The older population itself is getting older. In 1986, the 65–74 age group was 8 times larger than in 1900, and the 75–84 group was 12 times larger. However, the increase in those 85 and older was 22 times greater! Census officials predict that by the middle of the next century, one out of every four Americans will be over the age of 65. Pharmaceutical and technologic advances have been quite successful in prolonging our existence on earth, but not necessarily in extending the quality of life. Socio-cultural changes, disruptive family relationships, loneliness, loss of control and social isolation are now contributing markedly to stress related disorders in the elderly, and these problems will steadily increase. This was eloquently demonstrated in Stewart Wolf's masterful 30 year study of the inhabitants of Roseto.

These and other important aspects of the complicated problem of stress in the elderly are comprehensively reviewed by Dr. Humphrey in this volume. The first section contains the background information required to provide an understanding and appreciation of the dimensions and future directions of this problem. The second section offers useful advice and methodologies to implement stress management strategies for older adults. It explains how exercise, meditation, biofeedback, relaxation and behavior modification can be utilized in reducing the ravages of geriatric stress and regain some sense of control.

Stress is difficult to define because it differs for each of us. However, it is clear from all the avenues of research that the sense of feeling or being out of control is uniformly distressful. Elderly individuals are often institutionalized, simply because society no longer gears its requirements to the abilities and needs of older people. Studies vividly demonstrate that those who are permitted to exercise more decisions about their life activities are twice as likely to live longer than those who follow an arbitrarily prescribed regimen. Such individuals are capable of establishing a much deeper, richer and meaningful relationship with others, if they are given the opportunity, and also the tools and skills to facilitate this. Dr. Humphrey provides useful clues on how to enhance that process, and to enable the elderly to add life to years, rather than merely years to life. After all, everyone wants to live long—but nobody wants to grow old.

PAUL J. ROSCH, M.D., F.A.C.P.
President, The American Institute of Stress
Clinical Professor of Medicine and Psychiatry
New York Medical College

PREFACE

The inspiration to write this book derived from my experience in presenting lectures on stress to various older adult groups. The nature of their questions and the substance of their discussions convinced me of the stress information needs of this age level. Thus, the book was conceived not only as a source for helping older adults understand about and cope with stress, but also to provide detailed information for them about the subject.

Over the years I have conducted interviews/surveys on stress of such populations as nurses, athletic coaches, teachers, psychiatrists and members of the United States Congress. Data for these surveys were collected with my own Humphrey Stress Inquiry Form. As a part of the data base for the present volume, my survey form was submitted to over 600 adults in the 65–85 year old age range. Although the stress concept is pretty much the same for any age level, my surveys and interviews provided me with specific stress needs and interests of older adults.

The book is organized into two parts. Part I consists of four chapters that are concerned with providing information that will assist the reader to understand better the complex and complicated subject of stress. The six chapters that comprise Part II are intended to set forth various procedures that older adults might use in dealing with stress.

The introductory chapter considers some of the characteristics of older adults and an attempt is made to dispel some of the false notions that some younger persons have about those in the upper age ranges.

In Chapter 2 the meaning of stress and other terms associated with it are discussed to help facilitate the communication problem when discussing the subject of stress.

The third chapter goes into detail about the concept of stress as well as consideration of the causes and effects of it.

In Chapter 4, the subject of emotion is discussed in terms of types of emotional patterns, emotional stability and how to deal with certain kinds of emotional experiences.

Chapter 5 gives an overview of stress management for older adults with reference to principles of living and a lifestyle that not only can help one deal with stress but possibly avoid it as well.

In Chapter 6, exercise is dealt with in terms of its benefits for older adults, how it can reduce stress and how older adults can plan their own exercise program.

Relaxation, the topic of Chapter 7 discusses progressive relaxation, mental practice and imagery in relaxation and how to proceed with deep muscle relaxation of the various muscle groups.

Chapter 8 is concerned with various types of meditation along with a procedure for meditating.

In Chapter 9, the practice of biofeedback is discussed along with various instruments used for this procedure.

In the final chapter, behavior modification is taken into account with procedures explained for its use. Examples of cases of behavior modification of older adults in reducing stress are presented.

A book is seldom the product of the author alone. Admittedly, the author does most of the things concerned with actually putting a book together. However, it is almost always true that many individuals participate, at least indirectly, in some way before a book is finally "put to bed." This volume is no exception.

To acknowledge everyone personally would be practically impossible. For example, there were over 600 older adults who participated in my surveys and interviews in the acquisition of data which was pertinent to the book. I would like to thank them collectively for taking the time to provide this important information.

It is possible and practical, however, to cite certain individuals personally. To the late Hans Selye (generally known as the "father of stress") with whom I collaborated on certain aspects of stress research, I am most grateful for his inspiration in all of my writings on stress. And finally, my profound thanks to Paul J. Rosch, M.D., President of The American Institute of Stress, for evaluating the content from the point of view of an international authority on the subject of stress and aging.

James H. Humphrey

CONTENTS

STRESS AMONG OLDER ADULTS

PART I
UNDERSTANDING

Chapter 1

CHARACTERISTICS OF OLDER ADULTS

Personal labeling has become so commonplace in modern society that practically everyone has some sort of identification that distinguishes him or her from others. Such is the case with the various age ranges. Generally speaking, a person proceeds through such classifications as infant, child, adolescent, young adult and adult.

After reaching adulthood there seems to be little agreement on how to refer to one in a certain age range. For example, most standard dictionaries define *middle age* as the period of life from about 40 to about 60. Incidentally, a time when some males are said to go through a "midlife crisis." The extent to which such men suffer from stress is not entirely clear. However, it is interesting to note that this phenomenon has been studied objectively. For example, one study[1] examined correlates of developmental psychological stress for 36 married professional men (aged 39–50) who had at least one adolescent child. The subjects completed a questionnaire that included a sex-role inventory, a parent-adolescent communication scale, and an occupational values scale. Based on sex role convergence and role adjustment theories, two sets of predictor variables were hierarchically entered into a multiple regression equation, with a third set of variables entered to control for individual stressors. Midlife stress outcome was found to be influenced only by role adjustment. The best univarariate predictors of stress outcome associated with midlife transition were quality of the parent-adolescent relationship and marital satisfaction.

After so-called middle age there is little agreement on how to refer to one in a certain age range. Among others, one can be referred to as any of the following: oldster, senior citizen, old fogey, old geezer, old bat, old bag and on and on. And finally there is just plain old and eventually old old. (In general, persons over 65 are considered as elderly, those over 75 as old, and those over 85 as old old).

There is no question that we have a great deal of difficulty determining just what *old* is. Bernard Baruch, the late famous financier and government adviser who lived to be 94, once said that he considered a person old who was 15 years older than he. Certainly, this could be a valid criterion for one who is 70 and would like to feel "young."

Most of us have heard the old saying, "You are as old as you feel." In this regard on the occasion of his 95th birthday, George Burns, the venerable television and movie star, when asked how he felt, is reputed to have quipped, "Not any differently than when I was 94." So, if you want to know how it feels to be 94, then simply live to be 95.

Various organizations and agencies periodically provide demographic information about older people. In this regard, the *American Association of Retired Persons* recently released the following information regarding the older population:

- Persons 65 years or older numbered 29.2 million in 1986. They represented 12.1% of the United States population, about one in every eight Americans. The number of older Americans has increased by 3.6 million or 14% since 1980, compared to an increase of 5% for the under-65 population.
- In 1986, there were 17.4 million older women and 11.8 million older men, or a gender ratio of 147 women for every 100 men. This ratio increased with age, ranging from 121 for the 65–69 group to a high of 253 for persons 85 and older.
- Since 1900, the percentage of Americans over 65 has tripled (4.1% in 1900 to 12.1% in 1986), and the number increased over nine times (from 3.1 million to 29.2 million).
- The older population itself is getting older. In 1986 the 65–74 age group (17.3 million) was eight times larger than in 1900, but in the 75–84 group (9.1 million) was 12 times larger and the 85 and over group was 22 times larger.
- In 1986, persons reaching age 65 had an average life expectancy of an additional 16.9 years (18.6 years for females and 14.8 years for males).
- A child born in 1986 could expect to live 74.9 years, about 28 years longer than a child born in 1900. The major part of this increase occurred because of reduced death rates of children and young adults.
- About 2.1 million persons celebrated their 65th birthday in 1986 (5,900 per day). In the same year, about 1.5 million persons 65 or older died, resulting in a net increase of over 630,000 (1,750 per day).

No question about it, the older population is here to stay—at least much longer than has been the case in the past. By the year 2030 it is estimated that there will be about 65 million older persons, two and one-half times as many as 1980.

AGING

Many people, as they age, who understand little about the aging process often feel that something unnatural is happening to them. Others who believe in some of the old wives' tales think that there is a certain stereotype to which they must conform. Unfortunately, there is an old concept of aging that is still much too prevalent among some persons. That is, that aging and disease are intertwined. To be old has been equated with being diseased. Moreover, the aging process has been perceived by some as an inevitable declining. By narrowly defining aging in this manner, a perplexing problem arises. That is, according to this perspective, older persons are by definition "less healthy" than younger adults since their life expectancy is less.

Unfortunately, even some members of the United States Congress have tended to impose a stereotypical classification upon older persons. For example, in a content analysis of published congressional speeches, it was found that most members of congress used stereotypes when describing older adults. Interestingly enough, both negative and positive themes occurred such as, perceiving the elderly in poor health, as unable to change, living in institutions, to be financially well off, to make friends easily, and to be good listeners. Stereotypes were used by advocates who were promoting funding for the elderly as well as by those in favor of decreasing funding for them.[2]

It will be the intent of the following discussions to provide the reader with information that should dispel some of these outmoded notions.

The United States Bureau of Census describes its concept of aging as follows: Aging marks the inexorable running out of the biological time clock for the individual, given the limited life span of possibly 100 years for the human species. Although the aging process goes on steadily throughout life, the term most commonly refers to changes in later life, following the reproductive age period. Aging proceeds at different rates for different individuals if we define it in physiological, psychological, behavioral, or sociological terms rather than chronological terms. Physiologists will look for signs of aging in the loss of functional efficiency of various bodily organs. Psychologists will look for signs of aging in the decline in neuromuscular skills, learning ability, judgment, memory, and sensory acuity. Behavioral scientists and sociologists will look for signs of aging in the individual's disengagement from social roles and growing inability to live independently. For some, the signs of physiological deterioration or the ability not to function independently come earlier than for others, but they inevitably appear for all as time passes.

Demographically, aging is defined essentially in terms of chronological age. A demographic approach can be justified on the assumption that, for large populations, the aging process, functional age, and physiological age follow chronological age closely. It avoids the problem of fixing the "onset" of aging in the individual case, a task faced by the biological and behavioral sciences and beset with grave difficulties. Moreover, the demographic approach can take advantage of statistical tabulations made from censuses and population surveys for conventional age groups.[3]

THEORIES OF AGING

The precise reason as to why people age is a complicated and complex one. And, in fact, it is not entirely understood. Over the years an abundance of theories of aging have been set forth. For example, reporting in my series on *Stress in Modern Society*, Morse and Pollack[4] suggest no less than nine such theories. Upon examination of the many theories, it can easily be determined that there is a great deal of overlapping from one theory to another, and that they can all be combined and reduced to more or less simple terms in describing the process of aging.

Two theories of aging that have recently emerged are: (1) that our cells are programmed from birth to begin the aging process and, (2) that a complex combination of hormone, nervous-system and immune-system actions tells our bodies to begin to age. Some students of aging suggest that the aging process can be more easily understood if one views it from the perspective of the body replacing used up cells throughout life. As time passes, the rate of cell replacement is gradually but constantly receding. This process can begin at about the time the body has reached full growth.

As far as *stress* and aging are concerned, my friend, the late Hans Selye, who is generally known as the "Father of Stress," and with whom I had the good fortune to collaborate on certain aspects of stress research in the late 1970s, believed that *aging results from the sum of all stresses to which the body has been exposed during a lifetime.*

The aforementioned Morse and Pollack identify this as the "Wear-and-Tear" theory and that it is based upon the fact that all inanimate objects wear out. The theory indicates that aging is caused by some form of wear and tear or damage to the various body components, either by use of the parts (wear and tear) or by injuries to the genetic or protein-forming mechanisms ("biological insults"). The injuries can occur from heat, light, oxidation, radiation, chemicals, trauma, pressure, infection, diet, dissipation, or some other sources. However, against this theory is the fact that organisms do not wear out like cars. Living things have the ability to repair their parts, especially skin, blood systems, and liver. Nevertheless, some parts do die, and are not replaced (e.g., nerves and blood vessels) and repair mechanisms can be injured. Wear-and-tear cannot be the complete picture since even when animals are kept in ideal environments such as excellent diets, no injuries, and presumably no disease, they still age and die. However, there are some environmental agents which can reduce aging and increase longevity in animals. These include reduced food intake, increased intake of antioxidants, and methods to reduce body temperature.

Another dimension of stress and aging is that which is concerned with whether or not stress is more prevalent among older adults than those who are younger. In this general regard, one study[5] examined whether distress is more prevalent among older than younger adults using data from 476 adults over 65 years of age. Findings indicated prevalence rates comparable with or lower than young age groups. When these data were examined in regression analyses, the relative unimportance of age became more obvious. Such findings may warrant a revised perception of distress and aging, one that acknowledges that older adults are subject to similar degrees of psychological distress as younger aged cohorts.

EFFECTS OF AGING

As mentioned previously, determining exactly when an individual is old is not an easy matter. We have all known older persons who were "spry for their age." At the same time others appear old when they are in high school. Nonetheless, as one ages there are certain changes that ordinarily take place. The following brief general discussion will take a few of these changes into account. However, it should be clearly understood that we are referring to the so-called "normal" person and that all such changes should be tempered by individual differences that exist among all of us. Thus, the following should be read with this general frame of reference in mind.

In the process of aging, one's body may not have as much strength and endurance. In addition, there may be a decrease in simple reaction time and speed of movement. Simple reaction time is the time elapsing between a sensory stimulus and the response to it. Speed of movement is concerned with how long it takes to move the body or one of its segments from one place to another. An example would be applying the brakes of a car. One reacts and it takes a certain amount of time to respond, and then it takes time to get the foot from the accelerator to the brake.

The lowering of basal metabolism, the rate at which energy is produced may cause one to tire more quickly as well as to be more sensitive to changes in weather conditions. For women, child bearing capacity ends of course with menopause, but there are cases on record where men have fathered children at an advanced age.

Vision and hearing may become less functional but this can be compensated for with various aids. As far as hearing is concerned, although lower tones may be heard well by older adults, sometimes they have difficulty with higher tones. In this general connection, perhaps a distinction should be made between hearing and listening. Although hearing is the instrument for listening, the latter is concerned with auditory perception—the mental interpretation of what a person hears. This is to say that one may be hearing something but at the same time not listening to it. Such a reaction by an older adult could possibly be misinterpreted as a failure to hear.

There can be a slowing down in tissue repair and the same is true for cell growth and division. This is probably the reason why older adults are likely to "bruise easily." Also older adults are cautioned about falling because of the brittleness of bones. Incidentally, according to T. Franklin Williams, Chief of the National Institute of Aging, fracture of the hip is one of the most devastating and feared medical crises of older adults. For example, more than 90% of all hip fractures occur in individuals over 70, and by age 90, one in three women will have sustained a hip fracture.

Although some older adults can do almost as much as previously, at the same time periods of recovery may be longer. In sum, it should be made clear that the above factors should be considered as natural changes in the aging process and not necessarily a sign of failing health.

AGING, HEALTH AND DISEASE

With the advent of the science of gerontology (study of aging), much has been learned about aging, health and disease. We now have come to recognize that health *needs* and *interests* of older adults do not differ radically from that of other age levels. In a sense this is to say that old age is not necessarily accompanied by illness. In other words, disease is not a significant concomitant to old age.

The fact that many older adults are not necessarily afflicted by ill health is shown in my surveys that indicate that although some may admit to "slowing down," less than 15% of adults over age 65 are operating on a limited basis. This means that over 85% of the older adults that I have surveyed and interviewed enjoy reasonably good health. In addition, my studies show that the large majority of older adults consider themselves to be in a healthful state. Conversely, very few actually believe that they could classify themselves as ill.

It may be that being an older adult might well have certain healthwise advantages. As an example, although older adults are likely to acquire more chronic conditions than the general population, at the same time they may be less likely to have acute illnesses. It also appears that they may not acquire infectious diseases at the same rate as younger adults. Then too, they have built up immunity to some diseases that they have previously had. Not only this, but they can acquire immunity to other infectious diseases as well. This may be the reason why older adults, on average, tend to have fewer cases of the common cold than younger segments of the population.

Although it may be true that some diseases are more prevalent during old age, this does not necessarily mean that such diseases are due to old age. That is, some conditions such as arthritis and cataracts that are associated with old age are not necessarily caused by it. For example, in many cases a disease could get its start at any time during one's life. Incidentally, it may not be common knowledge that there are various instances of children suffering from arthritis. All of this should point up the importance of periodic medical and health appraisals for the purpose of uncovering unsuspecting conditions. Such a practice can partially assure that a potentially debilating condition, if not arrested, can at least be properly controlled. This is what is known as preventive health measures and it provides some degree of protection for some of the diseases ordinarily associated with old age.

AGING AND MENTAL FUNCTIONING

Contrary to some popular thought, the body part that tends to age the least is the brain, and this might be a reason for the old saying, "the brain is willing but the body is not." This can be considered one of the good features of old age because one can continue to engage in interesting intellectual pursuits even after the body slows down physically.

It is quite possible that aging has little influence on mental functioning, unless of course older adults allow this to happen. Sometimes older adults are depicted as having a poor memory or losing it altogether and as a consequence some of them accept it to be true. However, as far as memory and forgetfulness of older adults are concerned, if one were asked what he or she was doing on December 7, 1941, almost without exception there would be accurate recall because this date is identified as one of the most tragic in American history—the bombing of Pearl Harbor. (Of course, one glaring exception is that of the 41st president of the United States in a campaign address to a group of military veterans on September 7, 1988, proclaiming that date as Pearl Harbor Day. Interestingly enough and indeed unfortunately, this gaffe was passed off by some as more or less of a joke and one "political pundit" suggested that he only missed the date by three months).

The reason for such recall is that although the memory of many older adults tends to decline for things that have happened recently, this is not necessarily true for things that have happened in the past. Important events are likely to be stored in one's memory bank almost indefinitely.

Gerontologists tend to agree that when there is a lack of memory for recent events it is perhaps due mainly to a lack of interest and attention instead of lack of ability to remember. It is also felt by some that if there is a change in memory of older persons it may be in the direction of greater accuracy. Although older adults may not always learn new things or "catch on" as quickly as some younger persons, at the same time when something is learned they may remember it better and possibly more accurately. It should be pointed out that problems of memory are not necessarily unique with older adults. I have known younger, extremely intelligent individuals who have had poor memories. In fact, there appears to be little or no correlation between memory and intelligence. (As an aside, those of us in my profession have the luxury of being forgiven for memory lapses and forgetfulness because we can retreat to the safe haven of the "absent-minded professor" syndrome.) Also it is interesting to note that some research indicates that older adults may be more practical in their orientation to problem-solving than those who are younger. Rather than thinking idealistically, they may be more likely to consider the impact that a decision will have on others.

Among the various agencies that are studying aging and memory are the Memory Assessment Clinics, a private research group based in Bethesda, Maryland and the Laboratory of Neuroscience, a part of the National Institute of Aging. There tends to be agreement on such points as: (1) only about five per cent of people over age 65 suffer from acute memory disorders, (2) some older adults may have more trouble recalling isolated facts like names, and (3) that the brain's processes for storing and retrieving information may possibly slow down over time.

As far as the latter is concerned it is believed that incoming data in the form of electrical impulses cause transmitters and receivers to branch out from the brain's nerve cells (neurons) to form electrical circuits with nearby neurons. The transmitters and receivers relay information across the cell junctions, and chemicals called *neurotransmitters* are produced at the junctions to speed the electrical impulse along. One theory for why slowdown occurs suggests that as the brain ages, it produces fewer of these neurotransmitters.

In recent years some interesting research has been conducted in the area of stress and mental functioning in older adults. A sampling of these studies is reported here.

Studying the influence of problems with concentration and memory on emotional distress and daily activities in chronic pain patients, Jamison and his associates[6] examined concentration and memory problems in 363 patients up to 83 years of age in relation to emotional distress and interference with daily activity. The subjects were divided into two groups based on how much difficulty they expressed in concentrating and remembering things. A physical examination, a pain evaluation questionnaire, and a stress scale were then administered. Physician ratings of the subjects' depression and anxiety were also obtained. Results indicated that problems in concentration and memory were related to emotional distress, poor family support, and interference with daily activities. It was suggested that techniques to improve concentration and memory should be incorporated as part of the multidisciplinary pain program.

In another study involving the relationship of stressful life events to intellectual functioning in women over 65, Sands[7] used a ratio of crystal/fluid abilities to estimate intellectual decline among 112 65–92 year old women. Crystallized abilities were assessed with vocabulary and comprehension test and fluid abilities with the Block Design and Object Assembly subtests of the WAIS. The Schedule of Recent Events was used as a measure of stress along with a method of quantifying individual estimates of stress experience. In addition, the relationship of subsets of actual events experienced to intellectual functioning was analyzed. Stress was found to be related to the ratio used to estimate decline. Changes in personal health and changes in health of a family member were positively related and vacations were negatively related to decline in intellectual functioning.

In another frame of reference, history is replete with cases where individuals have made significant contributions to society in their later years. For instance, Grandma Moses did not begin work on her famous paintings until she was 78. Similarly, Clara Barton founded the American Red Cross when she was over 60 and served as its president until age 84. In more modern times the aforementioned George Burns has been in show business for over 85 years and Bob Hope continues to entertain appreciative audiences in his late eighties. The late Claude Pepper, in his late eighties was the recognized champion of the elderly and made many impassioned pleas in their behalf on the floor of the United States House of Representatives.

Unfortunately, not all older politicians are as astute as was Congressman Pepper. In fact, some of them have actually given old age a bad name, in that they are simply inept and lacking in competence. In spite of this, many younger members of the media, failing to recognize this ineptness and incompetence, continue to portray such individuals as suffering from old age. Indeed, old age should not be equated with such a condition when lack of ability is really the cause of inadequate performance. An effort will be made to clear up this misconception in the following discussion.

In one of my interviews with an 82-year-old woman she commented, "I have had a full and satisfactory life, but now I am—for the first time—afraid; not of death but of the approach of senility." How unfortunate that anyone in modern times would be led to subscribe to this outmoded idea. It is true that at one time it was thought that what was called "senility" was caused by the physical deterioration of the brain. It is now believed that if such deterioration occurs it is likely to be caused by illness or an injury and not by aging. Although the term *senility* was once used to describe the condition of physical and/or mental infirmity of old age, the term has fallen into disrepute among gerontologists and many members of the medical community. Among some gerontologists the term senility has been replaced by the term *dementia*, the current trend being to define a disease factor related to this condition such as Alzheimer's disease.

LONGEVITY

Simply stated, longevity means length of life or the number of years of life expectancy. For obvious reasons most of us are interested in length of life as well as how much longer we can expect to live.

It is interesting to consider life expectancy in the past as compared to the present. At about the time of Christ, average life expectancy was less than 25 years. By the 1850s this had risen to about 35 years and by the 1960s to a bit over 65 years. And of course due to modern medical advances and technology life expectancy continues upward at a tremendous rate. In fact, as soon as a prediction is made it is almost out of date. Incidentally, one estimate indicates that presently there have been over 50,000 persons who have reached 100 years of age and this is supposed to go up to one million by the year 2040.

With many persons living much longer than in the past, the sciences of *gerontology* and *geriatrics* have almost become household words. As mentioned previously the former is concerned with the study of aging while geriatrics is a branch of medicine that deals with diseases of old age.

It is recognized that heredity plays a significant part in the life length of some persons. For example, other things being equal people who have had parents and grandparents who lived long lives tend to have a long life span themselves. However true this may be, we are not able to select our ancestors. Nonetheless, at least some of us are in a position to have some control over the kind of environment in which we must function. This means that we should give serious consideration to such concerns as periodic health and medical examinations, practicing good nutrition, getting sufficient rest, engaging in wholesome physical activity and exercise, and, of course, avoiding undesirable stress. Although there is no particular formula that will guarantee that one will live to a "ripe old age," engaging in the above practices should go a long way in accomplishing this objective.

Chapter 2

THE STRESS TERMINOLOGY PROBLEM

There is an unbelievable amount of confusion surrounding the meaning of stress and stress-related terms. In fact, Dr. Paul J. Rosch, President of the American Institute of Stress, has commented: "Everyone talks about stress, and presumably everyone knows what it is—but in point of fact, no one *knows* what stress is. It not only means different things to different people, it *is* different things to different people.[8]

It appears important to attempt to arrive at some operational definitions and descriptions of some of these terms. If this can be accomplished, it will make for much easier communication in dealing with stress. It is the intent of this chapter to provide information that will help to facilitate communication in the area of stress.

An intelligent discussion of any subject perhaps should be concerned with some sort of understanding of the terminology connected with that particular subject. This means that we should be concerned with the language and vocabulary used to communicate about a given subject. Such is the case with the subject of stress.

There are several important reasons why stress terminology should be considered. For one thing, my review of several hundred pieces of literature concerned with stress has revealed that the terminology connected with it is voluminous, sometimes contradictory, and, to say the least, rather confusing. Moreover, a survey of several hundred older adults aged 65 to 85 has revealed that a great deal of confusion exists in this particular population with regard to the meaning of stress and stress-related terms.

Many times, terms whose meanings are different are likely to be used interchangably to mean the same thing. Conversely, the same term may be used under various circumstances to denote several different meanings. The resulting confusion for the reader is obvious, because such usage of terminology can likely generate a situation of multiple meanings as far as the general area of stress is concerned. In this regard, my interviews and surveys of various population groups, including older adults, have revealed a wide variety of understanding with reference to the meaning of stress.

(*NOTE:* At this point would you please take a piece of paper and complete the following sentence: Stress is _____.
The reason for asking you to do this is so that you can compare your answer with the results of my previously-mentioned survey of older adults about the meaning of stress. These results are reported in the following discussion.)

HOW STRESS IS PERCEIVED BY OLDER ADULTS

Since the term, stress, appears to mean so many different things to different people, I considered it appropriate to try to get some idea of older adults' concepts of it. This was accomplished by having several hundred older adults fill in the above sentence completion item. It is to be expected that there would be a rather wide variety of responses among older adults as far as their concepts of stress are concerned. In fact, "experts" themselves are not always in complete agreement as to its precise meaning. My consideration of older adults' concepts of stress focused on the number of times certain *key* words emerged in the responses. By identifying such key words, it was felt that a fairly valid assessment could be made of how older adults conceived of what stress means to them. The following list gives the key words and the percentage of times they appeared in older adults' concepts of stress.

Key Word	Per Cent
Emotion	23
Strain	16
Tension	16
Worry	16
Pressure	10
Anxiety	10
Adjustment	6
Frustration	3

These data were collected with one of the items of the Humphrey Stress Inquiry Form which was submitted to over 600 adults in the 65–85 year age range. Slightly over 500 older adults answered this item. The following is a sampling of these responses:
Stress is:

- Severe emotional and/or physical strain usually caused by conditions beyond our immediately control.
- Environmental conditions that produce internal disturbance in the attempt to adjust.
- The impact of emotional and physical occurrences over which one seems to have no control.
- The inability to handle daily problems without too much mental strain.
- Tension build up due to factors that are unknown causes.
- Pressure and anxiety.
- Mental and physical worry.
- Emotional problems and health.
- Anticipating fear and anxiety.
- The inability to handle problems without too much mental strain.
- When you are upset emotionally and you have trouble relaxing.
- Worrying about things you can't do anything about.
- Mental or physical tension or strain.
- Emotions in distress.
- Mental tension of being uptight.
- Emotions effected by unpleasant incidents.
- A feeling of anxiety over family.
- Problems that people worry about.
- Inability to adjust.
- Worry and grief.
- Pressure from physical and mental strain.
- Nervousness and tension.
- The impact of emotions.
- Is mainly mental anguish and tension.
- Pressure from everyday activities.

In summarizing the responses of older adults, two rather interesting bits of information emerged. First, there were relatively few who saw any aspect of stress as positive. That is, the responses were predominantly of a nature that conceived stress as always being undesirable with little or no positive effects. (Desirable stress will be discussed in the next chapter.) Second, in a large percentage of the cases, older adults' concepts of stress tended to focus upon the *stressor* rather than the condition of stress itself. This would appear to be natural because it has been only in relatively recent years that literature on the subject of stress has become more plentiful in terms of describing what it is and how it affects the human organism. At any rate, the responses of older adults about their concepts of stress provided me with certain important guidelines in preparing the content for this book. Because of this, the collection of such data was a worthwhile undertaking. (*NOTE:* Before reading further I would like to request that you compare your concept of stress with the survey results.)

THE MEANING OF STRESS AND RELATED TERMS

It should be understood from the outset that I am not attempting to develop a set of standardized stress-related terms. This would be almost impossible and, at the same time, probably impractical. The purpose is mainly for communication as far as this particular book is concerned. This is to say that when a term is used, the reader will know the meaning of it for purposes of this book.

In some instances, in the discussion of terminology that follows, I will resort to terms used by various authorities in the field and in others, insofar as they may be available, purely technical definitions. It should be understood that many of the terms alluded to have some sort of general meaning attached to them. An attempt will be made in some cases to start with this general meaning and to give it specificity for the subject at hand.

Stress

There is no solid agreement regarding the derivation of the term, stress. For example, some sources suggest that the term is derived from the Latin word *stringere,* meaning "to bind tightly." Other sources contend that the term derives from the French word *destress* (anglicized to *distress*), and suggest that the prefix "dis" was eventually eliminated because of slurring, as in the case of the word *because* sometimes becoming *'cause.* Writing in my first volume of *Human Stress: Current Selected Research,* Dr. Paul J. Rosch[9] gave the term an historical flavor in the foreword of that publication as follows:

Of course, stress had been employed in physics and engineering for several hundred years. In 1676, Hooke's Law described the effect of *stresses,* or loads, that produced various degrees of *strain,* or distortion, on different materials depending on their coefficient of elasticity.

Selye once complained to me that had his knowledge of English been more precise, he might have labeled his hypothesis the "strain concept," and he did encounter all sorts of problems when his research had to be translated into foreign languages. In the late 1940s, when Selye was invited to give a series of lectures at the College de France, the academicians there had a great deal of difficulty finding a suitable word or phrase to describe this new entity. Consequently, a new word had to be created. And so *le stress* was born, quickly followed by *el stress, der stress, lo stress,* with similar neologism in Russian, Chinese, Japanese, and so forth.

A common generalized literal description of the term, stress, is a "constraining force or influence." When applied to the human organism, this could be interpreted to mean the extent to which the body can withstand a given force or influence. In this regard, one of the most often quoted descriptions of stress is that of Selye who described it as the "nonspecific response of the body to any demand made upon it." This means that stress involves a mobilization of the bodily resources in response to some sort of stimulus (stressor). These responses can include various physical and chemical changes in the organism. (Selye's concept will be explained in more detail in the following chapter.) This description of stress could be extended by saying that it involves demands that tax and/or exceed the resources of the human organism. This means that stress not only involves these bodily responses, but that it also involves wear and tear on the organism brought about by these responses. In essence, stress can be considered as any factor acting internally or externally that makes it difficult to adapt and that induces increased effort on the part of a person to maintain a state of equilibrium within himself and with his external environment.

Tension

The term, tension, is very frequently used in relation to stress and, thus, attention should be given to the meaning of this term. It is interesting to examine the entries for these terms in the *Education Index*. This bibliographical index of periodical educational literature records entries on these two terms as follows:

Stress	(physiology)
Stress	(psychology) see Tension (psychology)
Tension	(physiology) see *Stress* (physiology)
Tension	(psychology)

This indicates that there are physiological and psychological aspects of both stress and tension. However, articles in the periodical literature listed as "stress" articles seem to imply that stress is more physiologically oriented and that tension is more psychologically oriented. Thus, psychological stress and psychological tension could be interpreted to mean the same thing. The breakdown in this position is seen where there is another entry for tension concerned with *muscular* tension. The latter, of course, must be considered to have a physiological orientation. In the final analysis, the validity of these entries will depend upon the point of view of each individual. As we shall see later, the validity of this particular cataloging of these terms may possibly be at odds with a more specific meaning of the term.

The late Arthur Steinhaus,[10] a notable physiologist, considered tensions as unnecessary or exaggerated muscle contractions, which could be accompanied by abnormally great or reduced activities of the internal organs. He viewed tensions in two frames of reference; first, as *physiologic* or *unlearned tensions*, and second, as *psychologic* or *learned tensions*. An example of the first, physiologic or unlearned tensions would be "tensing" at bright lights or intense sounds. He considered psychologic or learned tensions responses to stimuli that ordinarily do not involve muscular contractions, but that at sometime earlier in a person's experience were associated with a situation in which tension was a part of the normal response. In view of the fact that the brain connects any events that stimulate it simultaneously, it would appear to follow that, depending upon the unlimited kinds of personal experiences one might have, he may show tension to any and all kinds of stimuli. An example of a psychologic or learned tension would be an inability to relax when riding in a car after experiencing or imagining too many automobile accidents.

In a sense, it may be inferred that physiologic or unlearned tensions may be latent as a result of a previous experience and may emerge at a later time. Although there may be a hairline distinction in the minds of some people, perhaps an essential difference between stress and tension is that the former is a physical and/or mental state concerned with wear and tear on the organism, while the latter is either a spontaneous or latent condition which can bring about this wear and tear.

Emotion

Since the terms *stress* and *emotion* are used interchangably in the literature, consideration should be given to the meaning of the latter term. (Recall that *emotion* was the most prominent keyword in older adults' concepts of stress.)

A description of emotion that I tend to like is one that views it as the response an individual makes when confronted with a situation for which he is unprepared or which he interprets as a possible source of gain or loss for him. For example, if an individual is confronted with a situation for which he may not have a satisfactory response, the emotional pattern of fear could result. Or, if he finds himself in a position where his desires are frustrated, the emotional pattern of anger may occur. Emotion, then, is not the state of stress itself but rather it is a stressor that can stimulate stress. (The subject of emotions of older adults will be discussed in greater detail in Chapter 4.)

Anxiety

Another term often used to mean the same thing as stress is *anxiety*. In fact, some of the literature uses the expression anxiety *or* stress, implying that they are one and the same thing. This can lead to the "chicken and egg" controversy. That is, is stress the cause of anxiety or is anxiety the cause of stress? Or, is it a reciprocal situation? A basic literal meaning of the term anxiety is "uneasiness of the mind," but this simple generalization may be more complex than one might think. A notable clinical psychologist, C. Eugene Walker,[11] points out the fact that psychologists who deal with this area in detail have difficulty in defining the term. He gives as his own description of it the "reaction to a situation where we believe our well-being is endangered or threatened in some way." David Viscott,[12] another authoritative source, considers anxiety as the fear of hurt or loss. He contends that this leads to anger with anger leading to guilt, and guilt, unrelieved, leading to depression.

Burnout

Some persons may become unable to cope with the physical and emotional trauma generated by the demands on their energy, emotions, and time. Current research, conducted on people-oriented occupations, indicates that some vocations in the human services are characterized by several built-in sources of frustration, that eventually lead dedicated workers to become ineffective and apathetic; that is, "burned out."[13] Persons who experience burnout may begin to perceive their job as impossible. They may start to question their ability. Feeling helpless and out of control, persons nearing burnout may tire easily, and may experience headaches and/or digestive problems.[14]

Depression

When the word, "depression," is mentioned to older adults, many of them will probably reflect back to the great economic depression of the 1930s. In that day if people were "depressed" they were likely to use such terms as being "down in the dumps" or "having the blues."

The term, *depression,* as used here is thought of as a painful emotional reaction characterized by intense feelings of loss, sadness, worthlessness, failure or rejection not warranted by an objective view of events. Depression is often a disproportionately intense reaction to difficult life situations. It may be accompanied by such physiological symptoms as tension, slowing of motor and mental activity, fatigue, lack of appetite and insomnia;[15] that is, some of the same symptoms accompanying undesirable stress.

Depression is the most common psychiatric complaint among the elderly and accounts for as much as 50% of all mental disorders in the aged.[16] Also, depression in the elderly is difficult to treat because often there may be real reasons for feeling depressed such as failing health, loss of relatives and friends and financial problems.[17]

So much for terminology. Although the above brief discussion of certain terms does not exhaust the vocabulary used in relation to stress, it is hoped that it will serve in part to help the reader distinguish the use of terms basic to an understanding of the general area of stress. Other terminology will be described as needed when dealing with certain specific topics in subsequent discussions in the book.

Chapter 3

ABOUT STRESS

Although courses in stress are among the most popular of the health-related courses offered in college, it is unlikely that most older adults have much formal education on the subject. For this reason and because of the fact that my extensive surveys of older adults showed a considerable lack of knowledge about the stress concept, it seems important to present an overview of stressology—the study of stress. Thus, an attempt will be made to develop a relatively simplified discussion concerned with this phenomenon.

THEORIES OF STRESS

It should be mentioned that it is not the intent to get into a highly technical discourse on the very intricate aspects of stress. However, there are certain basic understandings that need to be taken into account, and this requires the use of certain technical terms. For this reason, it appears appropriate to provide an "on-the-spot" glossary of terms used in the discussion to follow.

ACTH —(Adreno Cortico Tropic Hormone) secreted by the pituitary gland. It influences the function of the adrenals and other glands in the body.

ADRENALIN —A hormone secreted by the medulla of the adrenal glands.

ADRENALS —Two glands in the upper posterior of the abdomen that produce and secrete hormones. They have two parts, the outer layer, called the *cortex* and the inner core called the *medulla.*

CORTICOIDS —Hormones produced by the adrenal cortex, an example of which is *cortisone.*

ENDOCRINE —Glands that secrete their hormones into the blood stream.

HYPOTHALAMUS —The primary activator of the autonomic nervous system, it plays a central role in translating neurological stimuli into endocrine processes during stress reactions.

PITUITARY — An endocrine gland located at the base of the brain about the size of a pea. It secretes important hormones, one of which is the ACTH hormone.

THYMUS — A ductless gland that is considered a part of the endocrine gland system, located behind the upper part of the breast bone.

Although there are various theories of stress, one of the better known ones and one to which many others are anchored, is that of Hans Selye. I have already given Selye's description of stress as the "nonspecific response of the body to any demand made upon it." The physiological processes and the reaction involved in Selye's stress model is known as the *General Adaptation Syndrome* and consists of three stages of *alarm reaction, resistance stage,* and the *exhaustive stage.*

In the first stage (alarm reaction), the body reacts to the stressor and causes the hypothalamus to produce a biochemical "messenger" which in turn causes the pituitary gland to secrete ACTH into the blood. This hormone then causes the adrenal gland to discharge adrenalin and other corticoids. This causes shrinkage of the thymus with an influence on heart rate, blood pressure, and the like. It is during the alarm stage that the resistance of the body is reduced.

In the second stage, *resistance* develops if the stressor is not too pronounced. Body adaptation develops to fight back the stress or possibly avoid it, and the body begins to repair damage, if any.

The third stage of *exhaustion* occurs if there is a long-continued exposure to the same stressor. The ability of adaptation is eventually exhausted and the signs of the first stage (alarm reaction) reappear. Selye contended that our adaptation resources are limited, and, when they become irreversible, the result is death.

As mentioned previously, Selye's stress model which places emphasis upon "non-specific" responses, has been widely recognized. However, the non-specific nature of stress has been questioned by some. In this connection, reference is made to the early brilliant research of John W. Mason,[18] a former president of the American Psychosomatic Society. His findings introduced support of the idea that there are other hormones involved in stress in addition to those of the pituitary-adrenal system. Mason's data suggested that psychological stressors activate other endocrine systems beside those activated by physiological stressors such as cold, electric shock, and the like.

As in the case of all research, the search for truth will continue and more and more precise and sophisticated procedures will emerge in the scientific study of stress. Current theories will be more critically appraised and evaluated, and other theories will continue to be advanced. In the meantime, there is abundant evidence to support the notion that stress in modern society is a most serious threat to the well-being of man if not controlled, and of course the most important factor in such control is man himself.

REACTIONS TO STRESS

There are various ways in which reactions to stress can be classified, and, in any kind of classification, there will be some degree of unavoidable overlapping. In the classification, here I arbitrarily suggest two broad classifications as *physiological* and *behavioral.*

Physiological Reactions

1. Rapid beating of the heart, which has sometimes been described as "pounding of the heart." We have all experienced this reaction at one time or another as a result of great excitement, or as a result of being afraid.
2. Perspiration, which is mostly of the palms of the hands, although there may be profuse sweating in some individuals at various other parts of the body.
3. The blood pressure rises, which may be referred to as a hidden reaction because the individual is not likely to be aware of it.
4. The pupils of the eyes may dilate, and, again the individual will not necessarily be aware of it.
5. The stomach seems to "knot up" and we tend to refer to this as "feeling a lump in the pit of the stomach." This, of course, can have a negative influence on digestion.
6. Sometimes individuals experience difficulty in swallowing, which is often characterized as a "lump in the throat."
7. There may be a "tight" feeling in the chest and when the stressful condition is relieved one may refer to it as "getting a load off my chest."

What these various bodily reactions mean is that the organism is gearing up for a response to a stressor. This phenomenon is called the *fight or flight* response and was first described as an *emergency* reaction by Walter B. Cannon,[19] the famous Harvard University Professor of Physiology a good many years ago. The fight or flight response prepares us for action in the same way that it did for prehistoric man when he was confronted with an enemy. His responses were decided on the basis of the particular situation, such as fighting an opponent for food or fleeing from an animal that provided him with an overmatched situation. In modern times, with all the potentially stressful conditions that provoke a fight or flight response, modern man uses these same physiological responses to face up to these kinds of situations. However, today, we generally do not need to fight physically (although we might feel like it sometimes), or run from wild animals, but our bodies still react with the same fight or flight response. Physiologists point out that we still need this means of self-preservation occasionally, but not in response to the emotional traumas and anxieties of modern living.

Behavioral Reactions

In discussing behavioral reactions, it should be mentioned again that various degrees of unavoidable overlapping may occur between these reactions and physiological reactions. Although behavioral reactions are, for the most part, physically oriented, they are likely to involve more overt manifestations than are provoked by the physiological reactions. For purposes of this discussion I will consider *behavior* to mean anything that one does as a result of some sort of stimulation.

A person under stress will function with a behavior that is different from ordinary behavior. I will arbitrarily subclassify these as: (1) *counter* behavior (sometimes referred to as defensive behavior), (2) *dysfunctional* behavior, and (3) *overt* behavior (sometimes referred to as expressive behavior).

In *counter behavior,* a person will sometimes take action that is intended to counteract the stressful situation. An example is an individual taking a defensive position; that is, a person practicing an "on-the-spot" relaxation technique, but at the same time, being unaware of it. He may take a deep breath and silently "count to ten" before taking action, if any.

Dysfunctional behavior means that a person will react in a manner that demonstrates impaired or abnormal functioning, which results in a lower level of skill performance than he is ordinarily capable of accomplishing. There may be changes in the normal speech patterns, and there may be a temporary loss of memory. Many of us have experienced this at one time or another due to a stress-inducing situation, with a "mental block" causing some degree of frustration while we attempt to get back on the original train of thought.

Overt behavior involves such reactions as distorted facial expressions (e. g., tics and twitches and biting the lip). There appears to be a need for a person to move about, and thus, pacing around is characteristic of this condition. Incidentally, there is a point of view that suggests that overt behavior in the form of activity is preferable for most individuals in most stressful situations, and can be highly effective in reducing threat and distress.

CLASSIFICATIONS OF STRESS

The difficulty encountered in attempting to devise a foolproof classification for the various kinds of stress should be obvious. The reason for this, of course, lies in the fact that it is practically impossible to fit a given type of stress into one exclusive category because of the possibilities of overlapping. However, an attempt will be made to do so, and, as mentioned before, any such classification on my part is purely arbitrary. Others may wish to make different classifications than those used here and, in the absence of anything resembling standardization, it is certainly their prerogative to do so. With this idea in mind, some general classifications of stress that will be dealt with in the following discussions are (1) desirable and undesirable stress, (2) physical stress, (3) psychological stress, and (4) social stress. It should be understood that this does not exhaust the possibilities of various kinds of stress classifications. That is, this particular listing is not necessarily theoretically complete, but for my purposes here should suffice.

Desirable and Undesirable Stress

The classic comment once made by Selye that "stress is the spice of life" sums up the idea that stress can be desirable as well as devastating. He went on to say that the only way one could avoid stress would be to never do anything and that certain kinds of activities have a beneficial influence in keeping the stress mechanism in good shape. Certainly, the human organism needs to be taxed in order to function well, and it is a well-known physiological fact that muscles will soon atrophy if not subjected to sufficient use.

At one time or another most of us have experienced "butterflies in the stomach" when faced with a particularly challenging situation. Thus, it is important that we understand that stress is a perfectly normal human state and that the organism is under various degrees of stress in those conditions which are related to happiness as well as those concerned with sadness.

In the literature, undesirable stress may be referred to as *distress.* It is interesting to note that Selye referred to the pleasant or healthy kind of stress as "eustress," and to the unpleasant or unhealthy kind as "distress."

I have mentioned some of the desirable features of stress, but like any factor involving the human organism, most anything in excess is not good for it. Of course, this holds true for abnormal amounts of stress. When stress becomes prolonged and unrelenting, and thus chronic, it can result in serious trouble. In the final analysis, the recommendation is not necessarily to avoid stress, but to keep it from becoming a chronic condition.

Although both "good" stress and "bad" stress reactions place specific demands for resources on the body, does this mean that good stress is "safe" and bad stress "dangerous?" Two prominent psychologists, Israel Posner and Lewis Leitner,[20] have some interesting suggestions in this regard. They feel that two psychological variables, *predictability* and *controllability* play an important role.

It can be reasoned that *predictable* pain and discomfort is less stressful because under this condition a person is said to be capable of learning when it is safe to "lower his guard" and relax. Since periods of impending pain are clearly signaled, the person can safely relax at times when the warning is absent. These periods of psychological safety seem to insulate individuals from harmful effects of stress. Obviously, persons receiving unsignaled pain have no way of knowing when it is safe to relax and thus are more likely to develop serious health problems as a result of the chronic psychological stress.

The second psychological variable, *controllability* of environmental stressors, which is closely related to coping behavior, also plays a major part in determining stress effects. The ability to control painful events may insulate individuals from experiencing damaging stress effects. However, such coping behavior is beneficial only if a person is given a feedback signal which informs him that the coping response was successful in avoiding an impending stressor. Without the feedback of success, active coping behavior, as such, may increase stress effects since it calls upon the energy reserves of the body and leaves it in a state of chronic stress.

The research on predictability and controllability of stressful events may help answer why it is that people who seek out stressful and challenging activities do not appear to develop stress illnesses from this form of stress. In contrast, when essentially similar body reactivity is produced by "bad" stress, then stress-related illnesses can be the result. Perhaps "good" stress does not produce illness because typically the events associated with it are planned in advance (they are predictable) or otherwise scheduled or integrated (they are controlled) into the individual's life. However, even activities which are generally considered to be pleasant and exciting (good stress) can produce illness if the individual is not forewarned or has little control over the events. And unpleasant events (bad stress) may result in stress-related illness because they generally come without warning and cannot be controlled.

In closing this section of the chapter, I should mention that some persons have taken the middle ground on this subject by saying that stress is not good nor bad, indicating that the effect of stress is not determined by the stress itself but how it is viewed and handled. That is, we either handle stress properly or we allow it to influence us negatively and thus become victims of undesirable stress.

Physical Stress

In discussing physical stress, it might be well to differentiate between the two terms *physical* and *physiological.* The former should be considered a broad term and can be described as "pertaining to or relating to the body." On the other hand, the term physiological is concerned with what the organs of the body do in relation to each other. Thus, physical stress could be conceived as unusual and excessive physical exertion, as well as certain physiological conditions brought about by some kind of stress.

Although there are many kinds of physical stress, they can be divided into two general types. One is referred to as *emergency* stress and the other as *continuing* stress. In emergency stress the previously described physiological reactions take place. That is, when an emergency arises such as bodily injury, hormones are discharged into the blood stream. This involves increase in heart rate, rise in blood pressure, and dilation of the blood vessels in the muscles to prepare themselves for immediate use of the energy that is generated.

In continuing stress the body reaction is more complicated. The physiological involvement is the same, but more and more hormones continue to be produced, the purpose of which is to increase body resistance. In cases where the stress is excessive, such as an extensive third degree burn, a third phase in the form of exhaustion of the adrenal glands can develop, sometimes culminating in fatality.

I have said that physical stress can be concerned with unusual and excessive exertion. This can be shown in a general way by performing an experiment involving some more or less mild physical exertion. First, try to find your resting pulse. This can be done by placing your right wrist, palm facing you, in your left hand. Now, bring the index and middle fingers of your left hand around the wrist and press lightly until you feel the beat of your pulse. Next, time this beat for ten seconds and then multiply this figure by six. This will give you your resting pulse rate per minute. For example, if you counted 12 beats in ten seconds, your resting pulse is 72 beats per minute. The next step is to engage in some physical activity. Stand and balance yourself on one foot. Hop up and down on this for a period of about 30 seconds, or less if it is too strenuous. You will find that, as a result of this activity, your pulse rate will be elevated above your resting pulse. Even with this small amount of physical exertion, the body was adjusting to cope with it, as evidenced by the rise in pulse rate. This was noticable to you; however, other things such as a slight rise in blood pressure were likely involved and of which you were not aware.

Psychological Stress

The main difference between physical stress and psychological stress is that the former involves a *real* situation, while psychological stress is more concerned with foreseeing or imagining an emergency. As an example, a vicarious experience of danger may be of sufficient intensity to cause muscle tension and elevate the heart rate.

It has been clearly demonstrated that prolonged and unrelenting nervous tension developing from psychological stress can result in mental anguish, which in turn can cause various serious problems.

It should be mentioned that physiological and psychological conceptions of stress have evolved independently within their respective fields.

Attempts are now being made to integrate these two conceptions. One writer on the subject, Ann Mikhail,[21] has proposed the following holistic definition of stress for the purpose of emphasizing the continuity between psychological and physiological theorizing: "Stress is a state which arises from an actual or perceived demand-capability imbalance in the organism's vital adjustment actions, and which is partially manifested by a non-specific response."

Social Stress

Human beings are social beings. They do things together. They play together. They work together for the benefit of society. They have fought together in time of national emergency in order to preserve the kind of society in which they believe. This means that life involves a constant series of social interactions. These interactions involve a two-way street, in that the individual has some sort of impact upon society, and in turn, society has an influence upon the individual. There are obviously many levels of social stress in life situations. For example, economic conditions and other social problems have been found to be very stressful situations for many people, older adults and their younger cohorts as well.

Negative attitudes about social interactions will almost always generate hard feelings and hostility among groups, making for more stressful conditions for all concerned. Also, a neutral or *laissez faire* attitude often degenerates into one of tolerance and, as such, can become almost as devastating as a negative attitude. In fact, the development of an "I don't care" attitude can often make life intolerable and bring about stress. In the final analysis, people themselves hold the key to the avoidance of undesirable social stress in any kind of environment, and good social relationships are most likely to be obtained if one assumes a positive attitude in such relationships.

CAUSES OF STRESS

A fair question to raise might be: What doesn't cause stress? I mention this because most human environments and society as a whole are now seen as stress-inducing to some degree. In recent years so many causes of cancer have been advanced that many persons have almost come to the conclusion that "everything causes cancer." Perhaps the same could be said of stress. Because it seems to have reached "near-epidemic" proportions, it is easy to believe that "everything causes stress."

A number of researchers have studied certain *life events* as causes of stress. They have attempted to find out what kinds of health problems are associated with various events, normal and abnormal, that occur to people either in the normal course of events or as a result of some sort of misfortune. One of the best known studies is that of Holmes and Rahe.[22] Following is a list of their ten most serious life events causing stress.

1. Death of a spouse
2. Divorce
3. Marital separation
4. Jail term
5. Death of a close family member
6. Personal injury or illness
7. Marriage
8. Fired at work
9. Marital reconciliation
10. Retirement

As important as life events scales are as a means of determining causes of stress, they are not without their critics. Some specialists feel that rather than life events, a better measure is that which is concerned with day-to-day problems. Prominent in this regard is Richard Lazarus[23] the distinguished stress researcher at the University of California at Berkeley. He and his associates collected data on a number of populations on what he identifies as "daily hassles." Following is the list of hassles for one of these populations— 100 white, middle-class, middle-aged men and women.

1. Concern about weight
2. Health of a family member
3. Rising prices of common goods
4. Home maintenance
5. Too many things to do
6. Misplacing or losing things
7. Yard work or outside maintenance
8. Property, investment, or taxes
9. Crime
10. Physical appearance

With regard to daily hassles among the elderly, Miller and Wilcox[24] administered a hassles scale, an uplifts scale, and psychological and physical health scales to residents (aged 69–93 years) in a nursing home. Results indicated that hassles (primarily health related) were negatively related to psychological and physical health, while uplifts were positively related to these problems. Praying received the single highest rating on uplifts, followed by thinking about the past. Feeling safe was the fourth most commonly mentioned source of uplift, and laughing, socializing, and gossiping served as common uplifts.

EFFECTS OF STRESS

The same line of thought that prompted my comment: "everything causes stress," could be applied with the assertion that "stress causes everything." For example, Pelletier[25] has reported that a tragic consequence is that stress-related psychological and physiological disorders have become the number one social and health problem in the last few years, and, further, that most standard medical textbooks attribute anywhere from 50 to 80 percent of all diseases to stress-related origins.

Recently I reviewed the literature by various medical authorities and found that among various other conditions, the following in some way could be stress-related: diabetes, cirrhosis of the liver, high blood pressure, peptic ulcer, migraine headaches, multiple sclerosis, herpes, lung disease, injury due to accidents, mental breakdown, cancer and coronary heart disease.

One of the more recent findings has been that there is evidence linking stress and the body's ability to fight disease. Some studies suggest the possibility of immune-system malfunction under stress by comparing the infection-fighting capability of white blood cells taken from normal and severely stressed individuals.

INDIVIDUAL DIFFERENCES AND STRESS

There are a variety of classifications of factors of individual differences with regard to stress. I will comment on three of these: (1) the noxious stimulus factor, (2) the personality factor, and (3) the gender factor.

The Noxious Stimulus Factor

Some years ago, Harold G. Wolff,[26] in search of ways in which people react to stress inducing factors, gave serious concern to what was identified as *noxious stimuli*. These are the kinds of stimuli that can have a damaging effect on the individual. Wolff believed that a stimulus could be noxious for one individual but not necessarily for another. This is to say that, while one stressor may have a devastating effect on one person, it may have little or no effect on another.

The Personality Factor

Before commenting on personality, as it pertains to individual differences in stress, it seems appropriate to discuss briefly my conception of personality. Ordinarily, personality is often dealt with only as a psychological entity. I think of it here in a broader frame of reference, which is the *total* personality. I view this total personality as consisting of physical, social, emotional, and intellectual aspects. This conforms, more or less, with what is becoming one rather common description of personality, "existence as a person," and this should be interpreted to mean the whole person or unified individual.

There appears to be general agreement that personality can influence the way individuals handle stress. On the other hand, there is much less agreement regarding personality as a causal factor in disease. One specific example of this is the difference in opinion regarding the extent to which certain types of personality are associated with heart disease. A case in point is that which concerns the work of Meyer Friedman and Ray H. Rosenman,[27] who have designated a Type A behavior and a Type B behavior. A person with Type A behavior tends to be aggressive, ambitious, competitive, and puts pressure on himself in getting things done. An individual with Type B behavior is more easy going, relaxed, and tends not to put pressure on himself. With regard to these two types of behavior, Friedman and Rosenman state, "In the absence of the Type A Behavior Pattern, coronary heart disease almost never occurs before seventy years of age, regardless of the fatty foods eaten, the cigarettes smoked or the lack of exercise. But when this behavior pattern is present, coronary heart disease can easily erupt in one's thirties or forties."

This point of view has come under challenge by some, the main point of contention being that there is little in the way of solid objective scientific evidence to support the hypothesis. In fact, at one American Heart Association forum for science writers it was reported that scientific studies fail to show that stress causes heart attack.[28] In this connection, it is interesting that many heart specialists have noted that death from heart disease is on a downward trend and may be expected to continue. They credit this, among other things, to diet, control of high blood pressure, and particularly to exercise.

It is also interesting to note that a recent special symposium on the interaction between the heart and brain at an American Psychiatric Association meeting[29] Rosenman reported that a 22-year research project found that Type A's were twice as likely as Type B's to develop coronary heart disease. In addition, however, the highly competitive nature found in Type A people increases the likelihood that important warning signs of heart disease—such as chest pains—will be denied. It is maintained that Type A's also survive better than Type B's, and it is speculated that this may have something to do with Type A people's adeptness at denial. This is to say that once a heart attack has occurred, Type A people tend to deny their symptoms, and therefore they may be better at suppressing the health anxieties that often accompany recovery from heart attack. According to Rosenman, with less anxiety there is less adrenalin release and a greater feeling of control over one's life.

There is general agreement that one manifests his or her personality through certain behavior traits and characteristics. This being the case, if these traits and characteristics can be positively identified as being detrimental to one's health, it may be possible to modify behaviors that cause the problems. To date, research in this area is difficult to pursue, mainly because of the problem of controlling the large number of influencing variables. (Chapter 10 will go into detail with regard to behavior modification.)

The Gender Factor

From certain points of view, ours has been a "man's world" traditionally, although no one can say with any great confidence whether, on the average, men have been happier or have had greater satisfaction in life than women.

Although various theories have been set forth, we can only speculate as to the prehistoric factors that resulted in the dominance of males. Nevertheless, their physical superiority for various activities and freedom from the periodic restrictions of weaknesses imposed by femininity and motherhood in women were no doubt influencing considerations. Simone de Beauvoir once suggested that as man rose above the animal level and began to exercise control over nature by means of tools, woman continued to be more closely bound to her animal nature and her body because of her maternal functions, and the biological and economic conditions of the primitive horde must have led to male superiority.

These speculations aside, many successful efforts to diminish sex discrimination have been made over the years. Indeed, a phenomenon of modern society is the vast changes in female behavior and assertiveness in the female personality. And even though to date the Equal Rights Amendment has not received sufficient state ratification, we "certainly have come a long way" when it is considered that in the 16th century the Council at Macon decided by a single vote that women *did* have a soul.

From a growth and developmental point of view, while at birth the female, on average, is from .5 to 1 centimeter less in length than the male and around 300 grams less in weight, she is actually a much better developed organism. It is estimated, again on average, that at the time of entrance into school, the female is usually 6 to 12 months more physically mature than the male. As a result, girls tend to learn earlier than boys how to perform certain tasks of manual dexterity. In fact, in one of my own studies of preschool children, it was found that little girls were able to perform the task of tying their shoelaces at a rate of almost four times of that of little boys. And, of course, the life expectancy of females is appreciably greater than that of males. But these are *physical* characteristics. So, how about factors related to *emotional* pressures?

With the emergence of Geraldine A. Ferraro in 1984 as the first female to be nominated by any political party for the second-highest office in the land, certain questions began to be raised regarding the ability of women to cope with the stressful conditions inherent in such a high-level position in government. Let us examine the premise.

As far as individual differences in stress with regard to the gender factor are concerned, it is felt generally that, with the women's movement, more females will continue to become more susceptible to stress. Some writers suggest that there are signs that women's vulnerability is increasing as fast as their independence. A century ago, peptic ulcers were a women's ailment, by a ratio of seven to three. Then, as frontier rigors were replaced by industrial ones, life got easier for women and harder for men, and from 1920 to 1940, nine out of ten victims were male. But since the mid-century the incidence of ulcers in women is again on the rise.[30]

A point of view, with reference to gender differences in stress, is that of Marianne Frankenhaeuser[31] Professor and Dean of the Experimental Psychology Research Unit of the Swedish Medical Research Council. She contends that women do not have the same readiness as do men in responding to environmental demands by adrenalin release. She does not feel that this response is due to gender but more so to a behavior pattern that is common to men in Western society.

A study of gender differences in stress reactivity was conducted by Joy N. Humphrey and George S. Everly[32] in which they used a State Measurement Scale for the purpose of finding out from male and female college students how they generally felt while experiencing a stress response situation. In other words, the purpose of the study was to investigate the perceptual dimensions of stress reactions in male and female students. The study included a random sample of 200 male students and a random sample of 199 female students.

The study showed that males and females "perceive" different stress reactions. Of greatest disparity between the perceptions of males and females was the emergence of *gastrointestinal sensitivities* (such as upset stomach) exclusively among males and the emergence of an *aversive affective sensitivity* (such as feeling "high strung" exclusively among females).

The investigators felt that it was impossible to attribute any significance to the appearance of a gastrointestinal sensitivity among males and an affective sensitivity among females. However, they did speculate that socio-cultural factors may have been involved. The reason for this is that it may be socially acceptable for males to develop "executive ulcers." Regarding the affective sensitivity, generally speaking, males are taught to repress emotions, and many males perceive emotion to be a sign of weakness. Similarly, females have been traditionally taught that it is appropriate for them to demonstrate emotion. As this era of changing sex roles progresses it will be interesting to see if perceptions of stress responsiveness change as well. If cultural factors do indeed influence perceptions of responsiveness, one might be willing to speculate that, eventually, there would be a more homogeneous perception of stress reactions among males and females.

As far as gender differences in stress in older adults is concerned, some interesting information is available. For example, in my interviews

with older adults a question often raised was: Do older women suffer
more from stress than older men?

A serious stressor among some of the older women in my surveys was
one of *financial worries.* In fact, about twice as many women as men cited
this to be a source of stress for them. Moreover, this was the case of
so-called well-to-do women as well as those with low and average incomes.
They were concerned as to whether or not they would have enough
money to "see them through."

In this general connection the following interesting information was
reported at a recent meeting of the Older Women's League:

• Despite the "myth of the wealthy elderly," the nation's women age 65
or older fare worse economically than their male counterparts.

• In general, older women are poorer, those who work have worse
jobs, are paid less, have worse pensions and worse medical coverage and
are more obligated to care for family members who are ill or disabled.

• Older women are less likely to reap the economic benefits from a
lifetime of work and they are more likely to live in poverty and isolation.

• Rather than being cared for, they are likely to continue to sacrifice
their health and their livelihood to care for others.

• About 15% of older women fall below the government's official
poverty line. The figure for older men is less than half as high.

• On the average if women become widowed, divorced or separated in
old age or if they are already single, they lack resources and health and
pension benefits equal to those of men.

• As one example of financial income, a typical male in the age range
of 65–69 averages more than 27% in social security benefits than do
women in the same age range. As far as pension benefits are concerned
males average over 45% more monthly than do women.

Generally speaking, according to this report there is ample reason for
the average older women to consider financial problems as a serious
source of stress.

In an interesting study, Cochran and Hale[33] examined gender differences in the relationship between health and psychological distress levels
in 53 males and 53 females in the 63–84 year old age range. They
administered a health self-rating scale and the Brief Symptom Inventory.
Results suggested that health plays a larger role in the psychological
stress levels of male than female older adults. Moreover, the connection
between health and anxiety seemed relatively pronounced for males and
almost negligible for females.

In another report Levy[34] reviewed findings that supported the conclusion that adult women across all age categories are more distressed than their male counterparts although the source of this distress may differ for middle-age and older women cohorts. Underlying the disturbance for the middle-aged woman are role loss, lack of marketable skills, and general inability to "break into" the larger social arena. For elderly women, the key issue underlying mood and behavioral dysfunction is identified as social isolation.

In summary, it has been the purpose of this chapter to present a general overview of some of the various aspects of stress. The following chapter will take into account some of the concerns that older adults need to contend with when dealing with the emotions.

Chapter 4

DEALING WITH EMOTIONS

In introducing the subject of emotions we are confronted with the fact that, for many years, it has been a difficult concept to define and, in addition, there have been many changing ideas and theories as far as the study of emotion is concerned. Obviously, it is not the purpose of a book of this nature to attempt to go into any great depth on a subject that has been one of the most intricate undertakings of psychology for many years. However, a general overview of the subject appears to be in order to help the reader have a clearer understanding of the emotional aspect of personality, particularly with regard to its involvement in stress.

Emotional stress can be brought about by the stimulus of any of the emotional patterns. For example, the emotional pattern of anger can be stimulated by such factors as the thwarting of one's wishes, or a number of cumulative irritations. Response to such stimuli can be either *impulsive* or *inhibited.* An impulsive expression of anger is one that is directed against a person or an object, while the inhibited expressions are kept under control, and may be manifested by such overt behaviors as skin flushing.

Generally speaking, emotional patterns can be placed into the two broad categories of *pleasant* emotions and *unpleasant* emotions. Pleasant emotional patterns include such things as joy, affection, happiness, and love—in the broad sense, while included among the unpleasant emotional patterns are anger, sorrow, jealousy, fear, and worry—an imaginary form of fear.

It is interesting to note that a good proportion of the literature is devoted to emotions that are unpleasant. It has been found that, in most basic psychology books, much more space is given to such emotional patterns as fear, hate, and guilt, than to such pleasant emotions as love, sympathy, and contentment.

At one time or another all of us have manifested emotional behavior as well as ordinary behavior. Differences in the structure of the organism and in the environment will largely govern the degree to which each individual expresses emotional behavior. Moreover, it has been suggested that the pleasantness or unpleasantness of an emotion seems to be determined by its strength or intensity, by the nature of the situation arousing it, and by the way the individual perceives or interprets the situation.

The ancient Greeks identified emotions with certain organs of the body. In general, sorrow was expressed from the heart (a broken heart); jealousy was associated with the liver; hate with the gall bladder; and anger with the spleen. In regard to the latter, we sometimes hear the expression "venting the spleen" on someone. This historical reference is made because in modern times we take into account certain conduits between the emotions and the body. These are by way of the nervous system and the endocrine system. That part of the nervous system principally concerned with the emotions is the autonomic nervous system, which controls such functions as the heartbeat, blood pressure, and digestion. When there is a stimulus of any of the emotional patterns, these two systems activate in the manner explained in Chapter 3. By way of illustration, if the emotional pattern of fear is stimulated, the heartbeat accelerates, breathing is more rapid, and the blood pressure is likely to rise. Energy fuel is discharged into the blood from storage in the liver, which causes the blood sugar to rise. These, along with other bodily functions serve to prepare the person to cope with the condition caused by the fear. He then reacts with the fight or flight response, also discussed in Chapter 3.

When attempting to evaluate the emotional aspect of personality, we encounter various degrees of difficulty, because of certain uncontrollable factors. Included among some of the methods used for attempting to measure emotional responses are the following:

1. Blood pressure: It rises when one is under some sort of emotional stress.
2. Blood sugar analysis: Under stressful conditions, more sugar enters the blood stream.
3. Pulse rate: Emotional stress causes it to elevate.
4. Galvanic skin response: Similar to the lie detector technique, and measurements are recorded in terms of perspiration on the palms of the hands.

These, as well as others that have been used by investigators of human emotion, have various and perhaps limited degrees of validity. In attempting to assess emotional reactivity, we often encounter the problem of the extent to which we are dealing with a purely physiological response or a purely emotional response. For example, one's pulse rate would be elevated by taking some sort of physical exercise. It could likewise be elevated if a person were the object of an embarrassing remark by another. Thus, in this illustration, the elevation of pulse rate could be caused for different reasons, the first being physiological and the second emotional. Then, too the type of emotional pattern is not identified by the measuring device. A joy response and an anger response will likely show the same, or nearly the same rise in pulse rate. These are some of the reasons why it is most difficult to arrive at a high degree of objectivity in studying the emotional aspect of personality.

FACTORS CONCERNED WITH EMOTIONAL STABILITY

Modern society involves a sequence of experiences that are characterized by the necessity for us to adjust. Consequently, it could be said that normal behavior is the result of successful adjustment, and abnormal behavior results from unsuccessful adjustment. The degree of adjustment that one achieves depends upon how adequately he is able to satisfy his basic needs and to fulfill his desires within the framework of his environment and the pattern or ways dictated by society.

There are many who feel that adjustment is a problem for older adults. In this regard, the following study by Grant[35] is of interest.

He examined the relocation stress hypothesis that older people find the move to a nursing home to be stressful, using archival time-series data. The prevalence of psychological distress following admission was obtained from nursing notes, written on monthly medical charts for 159 nursing home residents with a mean age of admission of 82 years. Excluding those with an organic psychotic disorder (19.5%), results showed that the majority of new residents (82.7%) were not distressed by the move. However, a large proportion of those who were stressed, and in particular those who had behavioral problems prior to admission, did experience psychological distress on admission, and this proportion dropped slowly over an 8-month period. This does not support the general relocation stress hypothesis of very old adults; however, it is consistent with a perceived control interpretation, focusing on alternative explanations for the behavior problems variable.

As mentioned previously, stress may be considered as any factor acting internally or externally that renders adaptation difficult, and which induces increased effort on the part of the person to maintain a state of equilibrium within himself and with his environment. When stress is induced as a result of the individual's not being able to meet his needs (basic demands) and to satisfy his desires (wants or wishes), *frustration* or *conflict* results. Frustration occurs when a need is not met, and conflict results when choices must be made between nearly equally attractive alternatives or when basic emotional forces oppose one another. In the emotionally healthy person, the degree of frustration is ordinarily in proportion to the intensity of the need or desire. That is, he will objectively observe and evaluate the situation to ascertain whether a solution is possible, and, if so, what solution would best enable him to achieve the fulfillment of his needs or his desires. However, every person has a *zone of tolerance* or limits for emotional stress within which he normally operates. If the stress becomes considerably greater than the tolerance level, or if the individual has not learned to cope with his problems and to objectively and intelligently solve them, some degree of maladjustment possibly can result.

It could be said that the major difference between you, as a normal older adult, and some criminal, confined to prison, is that you have the ability to control your emotional impulses to a greater extent than he. Perhaps many of us at one time or another have experienced the same kinds of emotions that have led the abnormal individual to commit violence, but we have been able to hold our powerful and violent emotions in check. This may be an extreme example, but it should suggest something of the importance of emotional control in modern society.

An important aspect of controlling the emotions is becoming able to function effectively and intelligently in an emotionally charged situation. Success in most life situations hinges upon this ability. Extremes of emotional upset must be avoided if the individual is to be able to think and act effectively. An unfortunate situation in modern society is that politicians and others sometimes try to get people to think with their emotions rather than their intelligence. Judging from many events that are occurring, they are having success with this approach.

It is sometimes helpful to visualize your emotions as being forces within you that are in a struggle for power with your mind as to which is to control you, your reason, or your emotions. Oftentimes, our basic emotions are blind and unconcerned with the welfare of other people, or sometimes even with our own welfare. Emotional stability has to do with gaining increased mastery over our emotions—not, of course, eliminating them—so that we may behave as intelligent and civilized human beings rather than as savages or children in temper tantrums.

In order to pursue a sensible course in our efforts to acquire desired emotional stability, there are certain factors that need to be taken into account. Some of these factors are the subject of the ensuing discussion.

Those factors concerned with emotional stability that will be considered are: (1) characteristics of emotionality, (2) emotional arousals and reactions, and (3) factors that influence emotionality.

Characteristics of Emotionality

1. **There are variations in how long emotions last.** A child's emotions may last for a few minutes and then terminate rather abruptly. The child gets it "out of his system" so to speak by expressing it outwardly. In contrast, some adult emotions may be long and drawn out. As children get older, expressing the emotions by overt action is encumbered by certain social restraints. This is to say that what might be socially acceptable at one age level is not necessarily so at another. This may be a reason for some children developing *moods*, which in a sense are states of emotion drawn out over a period of time and expressed slowly. Typical moods may be that of "sulking" due to restraint or anger, and being "jumpy" from repressed fear. Of course, it is common for these moods to prevail well into older adulthood.

2. **There are differences in the intensity of emotions.** You will probably recall in your own experience that some persons may react rather violently to a situation that, to you, might appear insignificant. This kind of behavior is likely to reflect one's background and past experience with specific kinds of situations.

3. **Emotions are subject to rapid change.** A young child is capable of shifting quickly from laughing to crying, or from anger to joy. Although the reason for this is not definitely known, it might be that there is not as much depth of feeling among children as there is among adults. In addition, it could be due to a lack of experience that children have had, as well as their state of intellectual development. We do know that young children have a short attention span, which could cause them to change rapidly from one kind of emotion to another. As we mature into older adults rapid change in emotions is likely to wane.

4. **Depending on the individual, emotions can appear with various degrees of frequency.** As individuals grow and mature, they manage to

develop the ability to adjust to situations that previously would have caused an emotional reaction. That is, no doubt, due to the acquisition of more experience with various kinds of emotional situations. As far as children are concerned, they learn through experience what is socially acceptable and what is socially unacceptable. This is particularly true if a child is reprimanded in some way following a violent emotional reaction. For this reason, a child may try to confront situations in ways that do not involve an emotional response. You probably know some adults who tend to react in much the same way.

5. **People differ in their emotional responses.** One person confronted with a situation that instills fear may run away from the immediate environment (hit and run driver), while another may try to hide. Different reactions of people to emotional situations are probably due to a host of factors. Included among these may be past experience with a certain kind of emotional situation, willingness of parents and other adults during childhood to help them become more independent, and family relationships in general.

6. **Strength of people's emotions are subject to change.** At some age levels certain kinds of emotions may be weak and later become stronger. Conversely, with some young children, emotions that were strong may tend to decline. For example, small children may be timid among strangers, but later when they see there is nothing to fear, the timidity is likely to diminish. This may be true of some older adults who experienced insecurity in childhood.

Emotional Arousals and Reactions

If we are to understand the nature of human emotions, we need to take into account some of those factors of emotional arousal and how people might react to them. Many different kinds of emotional patterns have been identified. For purposes here I have arbitrarily selected for discussion the emotional states of fear, worry, anger, jealousy and joy.

1. **Fear.** The term fear from the Old English *fir* may have been derived originally from the German word *fahr*, meaning danger or peril. In modern times fear is often thought of in terms of anxiety caused by present or impending danger or peril. For example, fear can generally be defined as a more generalized reaction to a vague sense of threat in absence of a specific or realistic dangerous object. However, the terms fear and anxiety are often used loosely and often interchangeably. When

fearful or anxious, individuals experience unpleasant changes in overt behavior, subjective feelings (including thoughts), and physiological activity.

Fears differ from anxiety in that the former are negative emotional responses to any specific environmental factor. But fears and anxiety are similar in the feelings they arouse: rapid heartbeat, sweating, quivering, heavy breathing, feeling weak or numb in the limbs, dizziness or faintness, muscular tension, the need to eliminate, and a sense of dread—the "fight or flight" response mechanism. Not all people experience all these signs of fear, but most experience some of them.

There are various ways of classifying fears. Spencer Rathus and Jeffrey Nevid[36] use the two broad classifications of *objective* fears and *irrational* fears.

Many objective fears are useful and necessary and it is logical that we be afraid of such things as: (1) touching a hot stove, (2) falling from a high place, (3) running into the street without looking for oncoming vehicles, and (4) receiving surgical procedures without benefit of anesthesia. These fears are said to be *rational* and *adaptive*.

Some fears are said to be *irrational* and *maladaptive*. It is an irrational fear when the objective danger is in disproportion to the amount of distress experienced. These kinds of fears are called *phobias* or phobic disorders, among some of which are: (1) fear of high places, though one may be in no objective danger of falling, (2) fear of closed-in, tight places when one is not necessarily in objective danger of being smothered or trapped, (3) fear of receiving injections—not because of the potential minor pain, but because of the "thought" of the procedure, (4) fear of working with sharp instruments, (5) fear of the dark, and (6) fear of being alone.

Irrational fears or phobias do not necessarily have to interfere with our lives. It matters little if you are afraid of heights if your life style permits you to avoid high places. However, some irrational fears can be debilitating experiences and interfere greatly with your attempt to lead your daily life. For instance, if one has no tolerance for the sight of blood or being in an environment of medical procedures, one may find his health or life endangered if he refrains from seeking treatment of an injury or disease. In such a case it would clearly be of benefit to do something about such fears.

In another frame of reference it should be mentioned that behavioral explanations of the development and maintenance of fears are based on learning principles. That is, basically it is assumed that all behavior, and thus the individual's fear responses, are learned from the environment.

Reporting in Volume 1 of my series on *Stress in Modern Society*, Whitehead, Mariela and Walker[37] suggest three paradigms by which learning takes place: respondent conditioning, operant conditioning and the two-factor theory of learning.

In *respondent conditioning* if a neutral stimulus is presented simultaneously with presentation of a fear provoking stimulus, the neutral stimulus will become a conditioned stimulus for fear. Thus, on subsequent occasions, the previously neutral stimulus will evoke a fear response. The classic experiment by Watson and Raynor[38] illustrates this process. In the experiment, a child learned to fear a white rat. Initially, the child, Little Albert, was shown the white rat for which he showed no fear. While the child was paying attention to the rat, he was frightened by a loud sound (striking a steel bar with a hammer held a safe distance behind the child's head). Following several repetitions of this, the child was noticed to be afraid of the rat. The original neutral stimulus (rat), therefore, became a conditioned stimulus to elicit fear. It was later noticed that the child generalized this fear to other "furry" objects (e.g., his mother's fur neckpiece). Watson and Raynor whimsically noted that a dynamically oriented child psychologist examining this child might produce many speculations as to the origin of the fear, but almost certainly would not state in his report that the child was obviously frightened by striking a steel bar behind his head as a white rat was placed in front of him — yet that is how the fear was produced.

Operant conditioning can account for the development of fear or the basis of reinforcement through the environmental contingencies that follow a fear response. For example, the child's fear of the dark may lead to much social reinforcement in terms of parental attention (including bedtime stories, snacks, and the like) at bed time. Similarly, a fear of bugs or dirt may make it "impossible" for the child to help pull weeds in the garden.

The *two-factor theory* was advanced by Mowrer[39] and both respondent and operant conditioning are embodied in this concept. According to this theory, fears first develop by respondent conditioning are maintained by operant conditioning. A neutral stimulus is paired with a fear-provoking stimulus and the neutral stimulus becomes a conditioned fear stimulus. The individual then engages in behavior which enables him to escape or avoid the conditioned fear stimulus. If such maneuvers are successful, they decrease the level of experienced anxiety or fear. This fear reduction serves to reinforce the behaviors that were instrumental in reducing the fear. For example, if a child is taking a bath and gets water in his nose, he may develop a fear of baths. In order to reduce the fear and anxiety, he may hide until just before bed time, fall asleep in the living room, or throw a tantrum when told to take a bath. The anxiety reduction experienced by avoiding the bath reinforces continued avoidance of baths.

In my interviews and surveys of older adults a great many forms of fear emerged. Following are the 10 most prominent of these. Fear:

1. Of growing older and "senility."
2. Of inability to accept change.
3. Of having an accident.
4. Of what evening news will bring.
5. Of where our country is headed.
6. Of lonesomeness.
7. Of being harmed.
9. Of not being accepted.
10. Of not getting enough rest.

2. Worry. It has already been mentioned that this might be an imaginary form of fear, and it can be a fear not aroused directly from one's environment. Worry can be aroused by imagining a situation that could possibly arise; that is, one could worry about other family members. Since worries are likely to be caused by *imaginary* rather than *real* conditions, they are not likely to be found in abundance among very young children. Perhaps the reason for this is that they have not reached a stage of intellectual development where they might imagine certain things that could cause worry. In many older adults, worry is a constant problem, and many will find things to worry about. Controlling worry is a difficult problem for those older adults who have problems in adjusting. In my surveys of older adults the following were the 10 most prominent worries. Worry:

1. About health.
2. About family members.
3. About adult children.
4. About lack of accomplishment.
5. About lack of money.
6. About time pressures.

7. About where I will live.
8. About the younger generation.
9. About being overweight.
10. About duties piling up.

3. Anger. This emotional response tends to occur more frequently than fear. This is probably due to the fact that there are more conditions that incite anger. In the case of children, they quickly learn that anger may get attention that otherwise would not be forthcoming (can you think of any "spoiled" adults who react in this manner?). It is likely that as children get older they may show more anger responses than fear responses because they soon see that there is not as much to fear as they originally thought.

Because of individual differences in people, there is a wide variation in anger responses, and as mentioned previously, these responses are either impulsive or inhibited. It should be recalled that in impulsive responses, one manifests an overt action against another person or an object, such as kicking a door. This form of child behavior is also sometimes manifested by some "adults."

Some of the things that were the cause of anger in the older adults in my surveys were:

1. Mediocrity in others.
2. Complaints of contemporaries.
3. Arguments.
4. Poor drivers on the road.
5. Waiting in line.
6. People trying to tell me what to do.
7. Unpleasant odors (smoke, paint).
8. Gossip.
9. That I can't drive.
10. Rock and roll music.

4. Jealousy. This response usually occurs when one feels a threat of loss of affection. Many psychologists believe that jealousy is closely related to anger. Because of this, a person may build up resentment against another person. Jealousy can be very devastating and every effort should be made to avoid it.

Jealousy is concerned with social interactions that involve persons that one likes. There are various ways in which the individual may respond. These include: (1) being aggressive toward the one he is jealous of, or possibly toward others as well, (2) withdrawing from the person whose affections he thinks have been lost, and (3) possible development of an "I don't care" attitude.

In some cases, individuals will not respond in any of the above ways. They might try to excel over the person of whom they are jealous. In other words, they might tend to do things to impress the person whose affections they thought had been lost.

The difficulty in obtaining information about personal jealousy by self-reporting should be obvious. Therefore, it was practically impossible to get any accurate accounting of jealousy that persisted among the older adults in my surveys. However, I suspect it would be essentially the same as for other age ranges and that it would depend upon individual differences of given personalities.

5. **Joy.** This pleasant emotion is one that we strive for because it is so important in maintaining emotional stability. Causes of joy differ from one age level to another, and from one person to another at the same age level. This is to say that what might be a joyful situation for one person might not necessarily be so for another.

Joy is expressed in various ways, but the most common are laughing and smiling, the latter being a restrained form of laughter. Some people respond to joy with a state of body relaxation. This is difficult to detect because it has little or no overt manifestation. However, it may be noticed when one compares it with tension caused by unpleasant emotions. Because joy can bring about a state of body relaxation and, thus, relief of tension, it is an excellent means of reducing stress. Persons who have a joyful outlook on life are likely to be the least stress ridden. In this regard, Bob Hope once credited laughter as being "good for the corpuscles."

Factors That Influence Emotionality

If we can consider that one is emotionally fit when his emotions are properly controlled and he is becoming more emotionally stable, then emotional fitness is dependent to a certain extent upon certain factors that influence emotionality. The following is a descriptive list of some of these factors.

1. **Fatigue.** There are two types of fatigue, *acute*, and *chronic*. Acute fatigue is a natural outcome of sustained or severe exertion. It is due to such physical factors as the accumulation of the by-products of muscular

exertion in the blood and to excessive "oxygen debt"—the inability of the body to take in as much oxygen as is being consumed by the muscular work. Psychological considerations may also be important in acute fatigue. That is, an individual who becomes bored with his situation, and who becomes preoccupied with the discomfort involved, will become "fatigued" much sooner than if he is highly motivated to do the same thing, is not bored, and does not think about the discomfort.

Chronic fatigue has reference to fatigue that lasts over extended periods—in contrast with acute fatigue, which tends to be followed by a recovery phase and restoration to normal within a more or less brief period of time. Chronic fatigue may be due to any and a variety of medical conditions (such conditions are the concern of the physician, who should evaluate all cases of chronic fatigue to assure that a disease condition is not responsible). It may also be due to psychological factors such as extreme boredom and/or worry of having to do, over an extended period, what one does not wish to do.

Fatigue tends to predispose people to irritability; consequently, we do things to ward it off such as "taking a break" at different times during the day. This may be a "coffee" or "snack" break. In this particular regard, some studies show that the hungrier a person is the more prone he may be to outbursts of anger.

2. Inferior Health Status. The same thing holds true here as in the case of fatigue. Temporary poor health, such as colds and the like, tend to make people irritable. In fact, there are studies that show that there are fewer emotional outbursts among healthy individuals than unhealthy individuals.

As far as stress and inferior health status of older adults is concerned, two studies reported here are of interest:

Roberto[40] explored the ways in which osteoporosis affected the lives of 115 community-dwelling older women aged 57–93 years, focusing on their levels of stress and adjustment patterns. Findings revealed that they perceived more stress in their lives since being diagnosed with osteoporosis than before the diagnosis. Pain, loss of roles, and other limitations placed on them due to their condition contributed to their feelings of stress.

Khorana[41] made a study of 60 inpatients up to 75 years of age with ischemic heart disease. It revealed that 65% had faced severe psychological stress such as financial pressures, deaths, and family problems prior to the onset of illness. When compared with 15 age-matched controls and the non-stressed patients, they had higher representation in higher socioeconomic status, Type A behavior and other psychomatic disorders.

3. **Intelligence.** Studies tend to show that, on the average, persons of low intelligence levels have less emotional control than those with higher levels of intelligence. This may be due to the fact that there may be less frustration if a person is intelligent enough to figure things out. The reverse could also be true because people with high levels of intelligence are better able to perceive things that would be likely to arouse emotions. Recall the previous discussion on thinking with the emotions rather than the intelligence.

4. **Social Environment.** In a social environment, where such things as quarreling and unrest exist, a person is predisposed to unpleasant emotional conditions. Likewise, schedules that are too crowded can cause undue emotional excitation among older adults as well as others.

5. **Aspiration Levels.** It can make for an emotionally unstable situation if expectations are set beyond one's ability. If one is not aware of his limitations, he (or others) may set goals too high, and as a result, have too many failures. Remember, worry about "lack of accomplishment" was the worry of the fourth greatest concern among older adults in my surveys. Many of those who identified this as a worry, put it in terms of not reaching their "aspiration levels."

All of the above factors can have a negative influence on emotionality. Therefore, efforts should be made insofar as possible to eliminate these factors, and those that cannot be completely eliminated at least should be kept under control.

GUIDELINES FOR THE DEVELOPMENT OF EMOTIONAL STABILITY

It is important to set forth some guidelines if we are to meet with any degree of success in our attempts to provide for emotional stability. The reason for this is to assure, at least to some extent, that our efforts at attaining optimum emotional stability will be based somewhat on a scientific approach. These guidelines might well take the form of *valid concepts of emotional stability*. The following list of such concepts is submitted with this general idea in mind:

1. **An emotional response may be brought about by a goal's being furthered or thwarted.** Serious attempts should be made by those responsible to assure successful experience in a given environment such as

home, job, or retirement resort. In the retirement resort setting, this can be accomplished in part by attempting to provide for individual differences within this environment. The environment should be such that each person derives a feeling of personal worth through making some sort of positive contribution.

2. Self-realization should be constructive. The opportunity for creative experiences that afford the individual a chance for self-realization should be inherent in a given environment. Individuals should plan with others to see that specific environmental activities are meeting their needs, and as a result, involve constructive experience.

3. Emotional reactions tend to increase beyond normal expectancy towards the constructive or destructive on the balance of furthering or hindering experiences of the individual. For some persons the confidence they need to be able to face the problems of life may come through physical expression. Therefore, such experiences as recreation in the form of pleasurable physical activity have tremendous potential to help contribute toward a solid base of emotional stability for older adults.

4. Depending on certain factors, one's own feelings may be accepted or rejected by the individual. All environmental experiences should make people feel good about themselves and have confidence in themselves. Satisfactory self-esteem is closely related to body control; physical-activity oriented experiences might be considered as one of the best ways of contributing to it. Sometimes self-esteem decreases in older adults due to a variety of factors. For example, in some cases a lower level of self-esteem can be generated by negative attitudes that some younger people have toward older persons. Other factors are concerned with a decline in social interaction and the power and control some older adults have over their environment. Situations that place a value on abilities of older adults, as well as to respect their right to make decisions go a long way in increasing self-esteem. Remember one of the things that caused anger in some older adults was: "People telling me what to do."

Research about older adults and self-esteem tends to show that engaging in an exercise program can be useful in elevating the self-esteem of older persons. For example, in one study[42] 23 persons in the 60–69 year age range participated in an aerobic exercise program. There was a control group of 19 persons ranging from 60–78 years of age. Those in the experimental group exercised three times weekly for 14 weeks while the control group continued their normal lifestyle. The study revealed significant increases in self-esteem for the experimental group. That is, they felt better about themselves as a result of the experience. (Chapter 6 will go into detail with regard to exercise, stress and older adults.)

OPPORTUNITIES FOR THE DEVELOPMENT OF EMOTIONAL STABILITY IN VARIOUS KINDS OF ENVIRONMENTS

Environments, such as the home, retirement resort, or job have the potential to provide for emotional stability. The extent to which this actually occurs is dependent primarily upon the kind of emotional climate provided by individuals responsible for it. For this reason, it appears pertinent to examine some of the potential opportunities that exist for the development of emotional stability in these environments. The following descriptive list is submitted for this purpose.

1. **Release of aggression in a socially acceptable manner.** This appears to to an outstanding way in which such activities as physical exercise can help provide older adults with opportunities to improve upon emotional stability.

2. **Inhibition of direct response to unpleasant emotions.** This does not necessarily mean that feelings concerned with such unpleasant emotions as fear and anger should be completely restrained. On the contrary, the interpretation should be that such feelings can take place less frequently in a wholesome environment. This means that opportunities should be provided to relieve tension rather than to aggravate it.

3. **Promotion of pleasant emotions.** Perhaps there is too much concern with suppressing unpleasant emotions and not enough attention given to promotion of pleasant ones. This means that older adults' experiences should provide a range of activities where all can succeed.

4. **Understanding about the ability and achievement of others.** In any educational experience emphasis can be placed upon achievements of the group, along with the function of each individual in the group. Group effort is important in most situations, regardless of where it might be.

5. **Being able to make a mistake without being ostracized.** In any setting, emphasis can be placed on *trying* and that one can learn not only from his own mistakes but from the mistakes of others as well.

EVALUATING INFLUENCES OF THE ENVIRONMENT ON THE DEVELOPMENT OF EMOTIONAL STABILITY

What we are essentially concerned with here is how an individual can make some sort of valid evaluation of the extent to which a particular environment contributes to emotional stability. This means that some attempt should be made to assess an environment with reference to whether or not these experiences are providing for emotional stability.

One approach would be to refer back to the list of "opportunities for the development of emotional stability in various kinds of environments" suggested in the immediately preceding discussion. These opportunities have been converted into a rating scale as follows:

1. The environmental experience provides for release of aggression in a socially acceptable manner.

   4 most of the time
   3 some of the time
   2 occasionally
   1 infrequently

2. The environmental experience provides for inhibition of direct response of unpleasant emotions.

   4 most of the time
   3 some of the time
   2 occasionally
   1 infrequently

3. The environmental experience provides for promotion of pleasant emotions.

   4 most of the time
   3 some of the time
   2 occasionally
   1 infrequently

4. The environmental experience provides for an understanding about the ability and achievement of others.

   4 most of the time
   3 some of the time
   2 occasionally
   1 infrequently

5. The environmental experience provides for being able to make a mistake without being ostracized.

4 most of the time
3 some of the time
2 occasionally
1 infrequently

If one makes these ratings objectively and conscientiously, a reasonably good procedure for evaluation is provided. Ratings can be made periodically to see if positive changes appear to be taking place. Ratings can be made for a single experience, a group of experiences, or for the total environmental experience. This procedure can help one identify the extent to which environmental experiences and/or conditions under which the experiences take place are contributing to emotional stability. The rating scale is useful for social directors and others in retirement resorts or other types of group living situations for older adults.

THE EMOTIONALLY HEALTHY PERSON

It seems appropriate to close this chapter by mentioning some of the characteristics of emotionally healthy persons. As we look at some of these characteristics we must recognize that they are not absolute or static. We are not always happy, and we sometimes find ourselves in situations where we are not overly confident. In fact, sometimes we may feel downright inadequate to solve commonplace problems that occur in our daily lives.

1. Emotionally healthy persons have achieved basic harmony within themselves and a workable relationship with others. They are able to function effectively, and usually happily even though they are well aware of the limitations and rigors involved in human existence.
2. Emotional healthy persons manage to adapt to the demands of environmental conditions with emotional responses that are appropriate in degree and kind to the stimuli and situations and that fall, generally, within the range of what is considered "normal" within various environments.
3. Emotionally healthy persons face problems directly and seek realistic and plausible solutions to them. They try to free themselves from excessive and unreal anxieties, worries, and fears, even though

they are aware that there is much to be concerned with and much to be anxious about in our complex modern society.

4. Emotionally healthy persons have developed a guiding philosophy of life and have a set of values that are acceptable to themselves and that are generally in harmony with those values of society that are reasonable and conducive to human happiness.

5. Emotionally healthy persons accept themselves and are willing to deal with the world as it exists in reality. They accept what cannot be changed at a particular time and place and they build and derive satisfaction within the framework of their own potentialities and those of their environment.

6. Emotionally healthy persons tend to be happy, and they tend to have an enthusiasm for living. They do not focus their attention exclusively upon what they consider to be their inadequacies, weaknesses, and "bad" qualities. They view those around them this way too.

7. Emotionally healthy persons have a variety of satisfying interests and they maintain a balance between their work, routine responsibilities, and recreation. They find constructive and satisfying outlets for creative expression of the interests that they undertake.

This list of characteristics of emotionally healthy persons presents a near-ideal situation and obviously none of us operate at these high levels at all times. However, they might well be considered as suitable guidelines for which we might strive to help us deal with and possibly prevent unpleasant emotional stress.

PART II
COPING

Chapter 5

STRESS MANAGEMENT FOR OLDER ADULTS

S tress management is concerned with a *lifestyle* that enables a person to deal with and attempt to overcome problems of undesirable stress. It should be understood that underlying conditions causing such problems differ, individuals dealing with the problems differ, and procedures for dealing with the problems differ. It is the intent of this chapter to present a generalized overview of stress management. The suggestions made will meet with varying degrees of success with older adults who practice them. However, of utmost importance is the fact that a positive attitude towards life is an essential prerequisite for any kind of stress management program that is undertaken.

In recent years, a great deal has been written about how one should go about coping with stress. This includes both general and specific procedures for stress management as well as specific coping strategies and techniques. As mentioned previously, it is the purpose of this chapter to deal with some of the general concerns of stress management.

SOME GENERAL PRINCIPLES OF LIVING
TO APPLY IN STRESS MANAGEMENT

Obviously, there are no resolute standard procedures that are guaranteed to relieve a person entirely from undesirable stress. There are, however, certain general principles of living which may be applied as guidelines to help alleviate stressful conditions.

All life pursuits involve both *general* and *specific* factors. In the case of dealing with stress, there are certain *general* principles of living that are likely to apply to most individuals. On the other hand, there are certain *specific* procedures for coping with stress that may be used by an individual in terms of how these procedures might meet his particular needs. The present discussion is concerned with some general principles of living of dealing with stress that in one way or another can be applied to practically all individuals.

63

The term *principle* should be interpreted to mean *guide to action.* Thus, the following general principles of living should be considered as guidelines, but not necessarily in any particular order of importance. Moreover, it should be recognized that each principle is not a separate entity unto itself. This means that all of the principles are in some way interrelated and interdependent upon each other.

RINCIPLE: Personal health practices should be carefully observed

Comment:

This is an easy principle to accept, but sometimes it is difficult to implement. No one is against health, but not everyone abides by those practices that can help maintain a suitable level of health. Some jobs with their imposing schedules, may cause workers to neglect the basic requirements that are essential for the human organism to reach an adequate functional level.

Current thinking, which suggests that the individual assume more responsibility for his own health, makes it incumbent upon all of us not to disregard such important needs as diet, adequate sleep and rest, sufficient physical activity, and balancing work with recreation, all of which can reduce one's ability to cope with the stressful conditions inherent in our daily lives. Over 70% of the older adults in my surveys said they were abiding by this principle — at least they thought they were. However, when provided with information about certain health practices, this fell to below 50%.

PRINCIPLE: There should be continuous self-evaluation.

Comment:

The practice of constantly taking stock of one's activities can help minimize problems encountered in the various aspects of one's environment. This can be accomplished in part by taking a little time at the end of each day for an evaluation of the events that occurred during the day, and reactions to those events. Setting aside this time period to review performance is not only important to the achievement of goals, but it is also important to remaining objective. Those who take time to do this will be more likely to identify certain problems over which they have no control, and thus will try to make an adjustment until such time that a positive change can be effected. The particular time that this task is performed is an individual matter; however, it is not recommended that it be done immediately at the end of the day. A little time should be taken to "unwind" before evaluating actions that took place during the day. Less than 40% of the older adults in my surveys engaged in this practice.

PRINCIPLE: Learning to recognize your own accomplishments.

Comment:

One must learn to recognize his own accomplishments and praise himself for them, especially if such praise is not offered by others. This is generally known as "stroking," or "patting one's self on the back." In practicing this procedure one can develop positive attitudes and/or belief systems about his own accomplishments and thus reduce stress. All too often, many people "sell themselves short" and do not give themselves credit for the important things that they accomplish. Less than one third of the older adults in my surveys engaged in this practice. It is interesting to note that it was reported in the last chapter that worry about "lack of accomplishment" was high on the list of worries among my respondents.

PRINCIPLE: Learn to take one thing at a time.

Comment:

This is concerned with time budgeting and procrastination. Most persons are likely to put things off, and, as a consequence, frustrations can build up as tasks pile up. There is a need to sort out those tasks in order of importance and attack them one at a time. Proper budgeting of time can help alleviate procrastination, which in itself can be a stress inducing factor. Budgeting of time can help eliminate worries of time urgency and the feeling of "too much to do in too short a time." About 50% of the older adults in my surveys practiced this but many indicated that they had difficulty in doing so.

PRINCIPLE: Learn to take things less seriously.

Comment:

This should not be interpreted to mean that important things should not be taken seriously. It does mean that there can be a fine line between what is actually serious and what is not. Sometimes when people look back at a particular event they may wonder how they could have become so excited about it. Those persons who are able to see the humorous side in their various environments tend to look at a potentially stressful situation more objectively, and this can assist in keeping stress levels low. Over 70% of the older adults reported that they abide by this principle, indicating that the older they became the easier it is for them to do this.

PRINCIPLE: Do things for others.

Comment:

People can sometimes take their mind off their own stressful conditions by offering to do something for other persons. When individuals are helpful to others, in attempting to relieve them of stress, they in turn tend to be relieved of stress themselves. Research tends to show that persons who volunteer to help others often get as much, or more, benefit from this practice as those they volunteer to help. This even occurs in children because it has been clearly demonstrated that older children who have reading problems improve their own reading ability when they assist younger children with these same problems. It is not surprising that over 80% of my respondents practiced this principle because this appears to be a characteristic of many older adults.

PRINCIPLE: Talk things over with others.

Comment:

People sometimes tend to keep things to themselves, and, as a consequence, they may not be aware that others may be disturbed by the same things. Sometimes discussing something with a friend or spouse can help one to see things in a much different light. It is important to keep in mind that such discussion should be positive and objective lest it degenerate into idle gossip. This, of course, can tend to cause deterioration of a situation that is already at a low ebb. Remember that one of the things that angered older adults in my surveys was gossip. Over 70% of my respondents found this to be an important principle in their lives.

PRINCIPLE: Stress should not be confused with challenge.

Comment:

People often relate stress to producing tensions and therefore expect anxiety to result. Contrary to this, constructive stress in the right amounts can challenge a person and promote motivation, thinking, and task completion. Thus, recognizing stress as a natural phenomenon of life is no doubt one of the first and most important steps in dealing with it. About one fourth of the respondents in my surveys were aware of this principle.

A LIFESTYLE CONCERNED WITH PERSONAL HEALTH

There appear to be two general factors to consider with regard to stress and health. First, objective evidence continues to accumulate to support the idea that prolonged stressful conditions can be most detrimental to the health of some individuals. And, second, along with new and modern techniques of relieving stress are many traditional health practices that long have helped people gain better control of their lives and thus reduce the negative effects of stressful living. It is the primary function here to deal with the second factor in the hope that the discussions will have a positive impact upon eliminating, or at least minimizing the conditions concerned with the first factor. To this end subsequent discussions in this chapter will deal with what I call the *fitness triangle:* (a) nutrition, (b) body restoration, and (c) physical activity and exercise. (Two parts of the triangle will be discussed in this chapter, i. e., nutrition and body restoration. Physical activity and exercise will be dealt with in detail in Chapter 6.) Before getting into specific discussions on these areas, it seems appropriate to give some consideration to the general area of health.

The Meaning of Health

The precise meaning that one associates with the term, health, depends in a large measure upon the particular frame of reference in which it is used. In past years it was a relatively common practice to think of health in terms of the condition of a living organism that is functioning normally. This idea about health is one that is still accepted by many people— including many in my surveys of older adults. In subscribing to this particular concept these individuals tend to think of health predominantly as a state in which there is absence of pain or symptoms related to a poorly functioning organism. When thought of only in this manner, health is concerned primarily in terms of a state in which there is absence of disease.

In more modern times health is being considered more and more in terms of *well-being,* which is perhaps our most important human value. In considering health from a point of view of well-being, the ideal state of health would perhaps be one in which all of the various parts of the human organism function at an optimum level at all times. Although it is very unlikely that the human organism will ever achieve the ideal state suggested here, such a level is ordinarily used as a standard for diagnosing or appraising the human health status.

The old meaning of health that considered it primarily only in terms of absence of disease tended to place it in a *negative* sense. The more modern concept places more *positive* emphasis on the term. This is to say that the meaning of health is interpreted as a level of well-being also. It seems logical to assume that modern society's goal should be directed toward achieving the highest level of well-being for all of its citizens. The extent to which this goal is being attained is being challenged by some critics. One of the major reasons for this is that there are many deficiencies in health care in the so-called "land of plenty" with close to 40 million Americans having no health insurance.[43]

Health Knowledge, Attitudes and Practice

Any discussion of health should consider the three important aspects of health knowledge, health attitudes and health practices. Each of these dimensions will be dealt with separately in the ensuing discussion, but it appears important at the outset to consider them together for the purpose of a better understanding of how they are related.

In order to benefit from health learning experiences, it is most important that these experiences develop into desirable health practices. Thus, the ultimate goal should be in the direction of a kind of behavior that is likely to ensure optimum present and future health for the individual. However, before the most desirable and worthwhile health practices can be achieved, there is a need for a certain amount of desirable health knowledge along with a proper attitude in applying this knowledge to health practice.

Although it is obvious that *to know* is not necessarily *to do,* nevertheless, that which is done wisely will depend in a large measure upon the kind and amount of knowledge one has acquired. In the accumulation of health knowledge one will need to understand *why* it is beneficial to follow a certain practice. When one knows why, it is perhaps more likely that he or she will develop a desirable attitude toward certain health practices. If a person has developed a sufficient amount of desirable health knowledge through valid health concepts, and also has a proper attitude, then he or she will be more apt to apply the knowledge in health behavior. Moreover, one should be in a better position to exercise good judgment and make wise decisions in matters pertaining to health if the right kind and amount of health knowledge has been obtained.

Health Knowledge. A somewhat frightening lack of knowledge about health was revealed recently in a national health test. In a nationwide sampling, 46% of the population had a score of poor; 27%, fair; 14%, good; and 13%, excellent. Among other things, this test indicated that only a very small percentage of the population could identify even three of the seven early possible signs of cancer. This is certainly not a very encouraging situation in a nation that considers itself to have some of the foremost educational facilities in the world.

Knowledge about health is acquired in a variety of different ways. Some of it is the product of tradition, and, as such, is oftentimes nothing more than folklore. Certain popular notions about health-related matters that have long since been dispelled by the scientific community are still held by many people who have not, for some reason or other, benefited from modern health knowledge. In many instances I found this to be the case in my surveys of older adults.

Other kinds of health knowledge of sorts are derived in our modern society from the constant bombardment of the eyes and ears by mass communication media such as television and radio. Although some of this information may be valid from a health point of view, everyone should be aware that the primary purpose of many kinds of advertising is to sell a product, and that in consequence they claim results that are not always likely to be attainable. (The *American Association of Retired Persons* is making a serious effort to alert older adults about some of the false advertising and health frauds that are directed at older adults.)

Another source of health knowledge is the home. In fact, most of our important health knowledge gets its start in the home. Parents are our first teachers and, for better or for worse, what we learn from them, mostly without our being aware that we are learning it, tends to remain with us. A good home should contribute much to the health knowledge of its children simply by providing good meals, and a friendly, well-regulated, pleasant and recreationally challenging environment in which to grow up. Children from such homes ordinarily do not have to *unlearn* a lot of faulty ideas and unwholesome attitudes when they arrive at the next great potential source of health knowledge—the schools. It should be borne in mind that many children who grow up in homes in the inner city and some remote parts of the country do not benefit from good home experiences and thus their first source of knowledge is the school. (The above comments about health knowledge and children seems pertinent here because in modern times it is not uncommon for older adults as grandparents to be a part of the family structure.)

The scope of knowledge that one might obtain about matters related to health is almost endless, and obviously it would be well nigh impossible to learn all there is to know about it. However, there are certain basic concepts about health that should be developed by individuals at all age levels. Generally speaking, the individual should acquire knowledge pertaining to the direct basic needs of the organism, and, in addition, knowledge regarding the human organism as it functions in its environment. It is well to remember that education is a life long process and older adults should attempt to obtain the best health information available from valid sources.

Health Attitudes. Any discussion of attitudes requires an identification of the meaning of the term. Although it is recognized that different people will attach different meanings to the term, attitude, for purposes here attitude will be thought of as associated with *feelings*. We hear such expressions as "How do you *feel* about it?" In a sense, this implies, "What is your *attitude* toward it?" Therefore, theoretically at least, attitude could be considered a factor in the determination of action because of this feeling about something. For example, knowledge alone that exercise is beneficial will not necessarily lead to regular exercising, but a strong feeling or attitude might be a determining factor that leads one to exercise regularly.

It should be mentioned at this point that, contrary to abundant empirical thought, there is little or no objective evidence to support unequivocally the contention that attitude has a positive, direct influence on behavior. One of the difficulties in studying this phenomenon scientifically lies in the questionable validity of instruments used to measure attitude. Moreover, there is no consistent agreement with regard to the meaning of attitudes. Thus, the position taken here is one of theoretical postulation based upon logical assumption.

As far as health attitudes are concerned, they might be viewed as a gap that can exist between health knowledge and health practice, and this gap needs to be bridged if effective health behavior is to result from acquiring valid health knowledge. Let us consider as an example a person who has acquired some knowledge regarding the degree to which cigarette smoking can be harmful to health. Perhaps the person will have some sort of underlying feeling toward such knowledge. He or she may choose to disregard it because some friends have also assumed such an attitude toward it, or the person may feel that the evidence is convincing enough to believe that cigarette smoking is something that he or she can get along without. In either case, the person has developed an attitude toward the practice of cigarette smoking and may act in accordance with this feeling. It should also be mentioned that the person may not necessarily react in accordance with his or her true feelings because he or she considers it fashionable to smoke cigarettes so as not to lose status with friends who do. (I regret to report that this was a feeling of some of the female respondents in my surveys.) Whichever way the person chooses to react will be tempered at least to an extent by the consequences that are associated with the knowledge acquired about cigarette smoking.

Obviously, one would hope that the accumulation of health knowledge would be accompanied by a positive attitude, and that this attitude would result in desirable action. It is possible that only in terms of such a positive attitude are desirable health practices, and thus a better way of living, likely to result.

Health Practice. It was suggested previously that *to know* is not necessarily *to do*. It is a well-known fact that all people do not capitalize on the knowledge they have acquired. Perhaps many are apt to act only on impulse; actions of others are influenced to an extent by their friends. However, in a matter as important as one's health, it appears reasonable to follow a course where the individual weighs the facts and scientific evidence before acting.

Perhaps one might look at health practices that are desirable and those that are undesirable, or, in other words, those health practices that will result in pleasantness or unpleasantness. If one weighs knowledge in these terms, then perhaps one can appreciate better the possible consequences of certain health practices.

To change behavior is not always an easy matter. However, it is hoped that most persons will want to make a positive modification of their own health behavior after acquiring health knowledge and forming favorable attitudes. In the final analysis the individual will make the decisions regarding his or her own health practices.

Daniel Boone once remarked that "profit is born of risk." In modern society the converse might be true in terms of the risks that people tend to take in matters pertaining to health. As far as one's personal health is concerned, it perhaps becomes a matter of how much risk one is willing to take, and one's health practices are likely to be based on this factor. By way of illustration we will refer again to cigarette smoking and health. To my knowledge, it has never been demonstrated scientifically that cigarette smoking is in any way beneficial to the physical health of the human organism; on the contrary, there has been a great deal of information accepted as evidence from a medical point of view that indicates that smoking can contribute to certain types of serious diseases. Yet untold numbers of people, including some older adults, are willing to assume a dangerous risk in defiance of such evidence. After a person has learned about some aspect of health, he or she is left with an element of choice. We should hope to see a course of health action chosen that will involve a minimum of risk.

A LIFESTYLE CONCERNED WITH THE FITNESS TRIANGLE

There are three basic essentials needed to maintain the human organism at a reasonable level of health. These are intake and utilization of proper foods, adequate body restoration and sufficient exercise. I have already labeled this triad the *Fitness Triangle* and the following discussions will focus on how the first two factors can assist older adults in keeping undesirable stress under control. (As mentioned before, the third factor of exercise and stress will be discussed in Chapter 6.)

Nutrition

Nutrition can be described as the sum of the processes by which a person takes in and utilizes food substances; that is, the nourishment of the body by food. These processes consist of (a) ingestion, (b) digestion, (c) absorption, and (d) assimilation.

Ingestion derives from the Latin word *ingestum*, the past participle of *ingerere*, meaning "to take in," and in this context it means taking in food, or the act of eating. The process of *digestion* involves the breaking down or conversion of food into substances that can be *absorbed* through the lining of the intestinal tract and into the blood and used in the body. *Assimilation* is concerned with the incorporation or conversion of nutrients into protoplasm which is the essential material making up living cells.

The body needs nutrients or foods to keep it functioning properly. These nutrients fall into the broad groups of proteins, carbohydrates, fats, vitamins and minerals. (Although water is not a nutrient in the strictest sense of the word, it must be included, for nutrition cannot take place without it.)

Three major functions of nutrients are: (a) building and repair of all body tissues, (b) regulation of all body functions, and (c) providing fuel for the body's energy needs. Although all of the nutrients can do their best work when they are in combination with other nutrients, each still has its own vital role to play.

Diet

Diet is an all-inclusive term used to refer to foods and liquids regularly consumed. The question is often raised, "What constitutes a balanced diet?" Essentially one answer is that along with sufficient fluids, one should include foods from the four basic food groups. These are the dairy group, the meat group, the vegetable and fruit group, and the bread and cereal group. (As an interesting aside, about 70% of my older adult respondents were aware that a proper diet is important to good health. In spite of this almost 15% of them admitted to skipping at least one meal each day.)

A guide to a balanced diet has been prepared by the staff of the United States Senate Select Committee on Nutrition and Human Needs. This Committee spent a great deal of time on hearings and research and some of its recommendations are listed as follows:

1. Eat less meat and more fish and poultry.
2. Replace whole milk with skim milk.
3. Reduce intake of eggs, butter and other high cholesterol sources.
4. Cut back on sugars to 15% of daily caloric intake.
5. Reduce intake of salt to a total of three grams per day.
6. Eat more fruit, vegetables, and whole grains.

The above recommendations are directed to the general population. However, one important fact must be remembered, and this is that eating is an individual matter. The problem may not be so much one of following an arbitrary diet as of learning to know what foods and proportions of foods keep one functioning best. The body is capable of compensating for an imbalance in the nutrients that one fails to get if the shortage is made up within a reasonable period of time. In other words, it is not necessary to have an exactly balanced diet at every meal. Indeed, it is possible to miss meals—even to go for several days without food—and show no signs of malnutrition, (although, of course, I am not recommending that you do this). The important consideration seems to be in the quality of the total intake over periods of time.

The foregoing observations should not be interpreted to mean that one should be indifferent or careless about food choices. In this regard, the 17th century gastronomist, Anthelme Brillat-Savarin, famous for his book *The Physiology of Taste*, once said, "Tell me what you eat and I will tell you what you are." The more modern adage, "You are what you eat" could well have been derived from this old quotation.

It is absurd that some people are more careful about what they feed their pets than they are about what they feed themselves. This kind of thoughtlessness has given rise to the claim that Americans are at once the most overfed and yet malnourished people in the world. Any radical departure from one's diet should be made only under the guidance of a physician and/or a qualified nutritionist.

The above adage, "You are what you eat," has recently been brought more clearly into focus because researchers now know that our bodies synthesize food substances known as *neurotransmitters*. Prominent nutritionists tend to be of the opinion that these neurotransmitters relay messages to the brain which, in turn, affects our moods, sex drive, appetite, and even personality. This is to say that adding a certain food or omitting another could be just what a person might need. It is believed that when a person is stressed the body becomes less able to make use of protein. Therefore, the general recommendation is that after any kind of stress one should eat more lean meat, fish or milk products. Also, since stress depletes the supply of vitamin C and potassium, these should be replaced by eating extra portions of citrus products.

The diets of some families include too much of certain foods that can be potentially harmful. A case in point is the intake of *cholesterol*. Excessive amounts of this chemical component of animal oils and fats are deposited in the blood vessels and may be a factor in the causation of hardening of the arteries, leading to a heart attack.

There is no question about it, cholesterol has become one of the health buzzwords of the 1980s and 1990s. The importance of cholesterol as a risk factor prompted the First National Cholesterol Conference held November 9–11, 1988. This meeting was sponsored by the National Cholesterol Education Program Coordinating Committee which includes some 25 member organizations. This Conference was a somewhat unique forum in that researchers, physicians, and policy and program experts shared new knowledge and program successes in the rapidly changing field of cholesterol.

The universal interest in this risk factor is certainly justified by such estimates as:

1. Over 50% of Americans have a cholesterol level that is too high.
2. Only about 8% of Americans know their cholesterol level.
3. As many as 250,000 lives could be saved each year if citizens were tested and took action to reduce their cholesterol.
4. For every 1% you lower your cholesterol, you reduce your risk of heart attack 2%.
5. If your cholesterol is 265 or over, you have four times the risk of heart attack as someone with 190 or less.
6. Nine out of ten people can substantially reduce their cholesterol level by diet.

It should be mentioned that not all cholesterol is bad. Actually, there are two kinds of lipoproteins, low-density lipoproteins (LDL) and high-density lipoproteins (HDL). The former is considered "bad" because cholesterol it carries is associated with an increased risk of hardening of the inner lining of arteries. HDL (good) appears to clear excess cholesterol from the arteries while LDL (bad) can lead to cholesterol build up in the artery walls.

Physicians vary widely in their beliefs about safe levels of cholesterol and not too long ago a very broad range of 150–300 was considered normal. However, recently thoughts on this matter have changed radically. For example, the National Heart, Lung and Blood Institute has announced more stringent guidelines. That is, it is now believed that total blood cholesterol should not go over 200, meaning 200 milligrams of total cholesterol per deciliter of blood.

As far as older adults are concerned, it is interesting to note that more women than men have high cholesterol. In fact, the American Heart Association has reported that a surprisingly high number of women in all age groups have been found to have elevated cholesterol. Particularly, on average, women's cholesterol levels tend to rise after menopause.

It is also interesting that there is some degree of controversy concerning the elderly and cholesterol. Some experts are of the belief that borderline and high risk cholesterol levels should be higher for older adults and this is based on the notion that the elderly can tolerate a higher cholesterol level. On the contrary others believe that the same cholesterol risk levels for middle age persons might well be the same as for the elderly.

Diet and Weight Control

Remember that I reported in the last chapter that "being overweight" was among the ten greatest "worries" of older adults in my surveys. Incidentally, over 80% of these were women.

Basically, weight gain or loss is a matter of energy intake versus energy expenditure of the body. If one wishes to decrease body fat one can reduce caloric intake (which is most easily done by reducing the amount of high-energy foods) and increase energy expenditure (by means of physical activity). By doing both, one can lower the weight a given amount in a given time by less severe dieting than would otherwise be necessary to accomplish the same thing. Some authorities feel that it may be a mistake to make reducing a matter of "will power." As in trying to stop smoking, will power may set up a desperate struggle from which the habit is likely to emerge victorious. Or a substitute habit may be acquired, as in the case of the story about the man who gave up drinking altogether—and since has been a helplessly obsessive gambler. The wiser course might be to determine why eating has become of disproportionate importance in life and, as in the case cited earlier, discover what needs to be done about it.

Because dieting is the most popular way of controlling weight, it seems appropriate to establish general principles when one undertakes the practice. The following list of such principles might well be considered by anyone contemplating a weight control program.

1. Seek the advice of a physician and/or qualified nutritionist.
2. If fat is to be lost, the calories taken in must be fewer than those needed for the body's energy requirements.
3. The diet, though low in calories, must be adequate in all other nutrients so that intakes for these do not become dangerously low.
4. It should be recognized that losing weight is not easy.
5. Foods are not forbidden, but portion control is emphasized.

6. There should be a sensible balance of energy-providing nutrients.
7. The diet should be realistic and should not call for superhuman effort.
8. Exercise at the same time is recommended.
9. The behaviors and emotions that lead to eating should be examined, and advice sought to help the dieter control these.

Diet and Stress

With very few exceptions, writers on the subject of stress emphasize the importance of diet as a general health measure. However, the question to pose is: Are there any specific forms of diet that can contribute to the prevention of stress and/or help one cope with it?" (I have already mentioned how some foods might be used when one is under stress, and later I will comment on the controversy surrounding the use of the so-called "stress formula vitamins.")

One specific approach to diet and stress is presented by Dr. J. Daniel Palm,[44] who suggests that many stress-initiated disorders are related to problems that originate in the regulation of the blood sugar level.

Dr. Palm's theory, developed as an extension of the data derived from controlled research states that insufficiency of sugar in the blood supplied to the brain is enough of a detrimental condition, and therefore a stress, to initiate physiological responses and behavioral changes that develop into a variety of disorders. A deficiency of blood sugar which is known to be associated with a variety of disorders is seen not as a consequence of the disease but as a primary and original psychological stress. Behavioral changes may represent inadequate or inappropriate attempts of the stress-affected persons to compensate. It is believed that if stress from an insufficiency of blood sugar can be prevented, various kinds of abnormal behavior can be controlled. To eliminate this stress of a deficiency of blood sugar, a new dietary program is proposed by Dr. Palm. This diet is based on the metabolic characteristics of *fructose* (fruit sugar) and its advantageous use when it is enchanged for glucose or other carbohydrates which are digested to glucose and then absorbed. (Fructose itself is a normal constituent of sucrose, which is ordinary table sugar. It also occurs naturally in many fruits and constitutes half of the content of honey.)

Writing in my series on *Stress in Modern Society,* Morse and Pollack[45] caution that an excess of fructose can also be a problem. This occurs more from the ingestion of soft drinks and processed foods where the concentration of fructose is often higher than it is in fruits and juices. It has also been found that when fructose intake is raised about 20% of a person's daily diet (up from the average of from 10–12%), total cholesterol may increase over 11% and triglycerides are elevated slightly above 56%.

Practically all theories have enthusiastic proponents as well as equally unenthusiastic opponents, and this sometimes results in a great deal of confusion among many people. The fact that the human organism is so complicated and complex makes any kind of research connected with it extremely difficult. Nevertheless, scholars in the scientific community continue to make important inquiries into the study of human needs.

Vitamins and Stress

From an historical point of view, the realization that vitamins are basic nutrients stands as a milestone in the emergence of the field of nutrition as a scientifically based discipline. Unlike such nutrients as protein, fats, and minerals, vitamins do not become a part of the structure of the body, but rather they serve as catalysts that make possible various chemical reactions within the body. These reactions have to do with converting food substances into the elements needed for utilization by the various cells of the body. For example, vitamin D needs to be present if calcium is to be metabolized and made available for use in the blood and bones.

The vitamins with which we are familiar today are commonly classified as *fat*-soluble and *water*-soluble. This designation means that the one group requires fatty substances and the other water if they are to be dissolved and used by the body. Although a large number of vitamins have been identified as being important to human nutrition, the exact function of some of them has not yet been determined.

In countries such as the United States it should not be difficult for people to select a diet that is sufficiently varied to include all necessary vitamins. However, poor dietary practices can lead to vitamin inadequacy, and as a precaution many people supplement their diets with vitamin pills. Even though such a supplement may not be needed, when taken in small amounts the vitamins may do no harm. This is particularly true of the water-soluble vitamins in that if one gets more than necessary, they will pass right through the body. (Recently, some scientists have been disputing this claim, especially if water-soluble vitamins are taken in extra large doses.) On the other hand, some of the fat-soluble vitamins may be toxic and overdoses could render possible harm. Of course, extra vitamins may be prescribed by physicians for a variety of reasons ranging from suspected malnutrition, to chronic fatigue, and postsurgical recovery.

In recent years a great deal of controversy has emerged as a result of what has been called *megavitamin therapy*, which concerns the use of certain vitamins in massive doses—sometimes as much as 1,000 times the U.S. Recommended Daily Allowances. The proponents for megavitamin therapy believe that massive doses of such vitamins, particularly vitamin C, and in some cases the B-complex vitamins, will prevent certain diseases and very significantly extend life. On the contrary, opponents of the practice maintain that it not only may be useless, but in some instances harmful as well.

It is interesting to note that there is some support for massive doses of certain vitamins as an important factor in surviving stress. In fact, there is a special class of vitamins sold over the counter called *stress formula vitamins*. The formula for these is one that includes large amounts of vitamin C and vitamin B-complex.

Anyone contemplating utilizing a vitamin supplement over and above the U.S. Recommended Daily Allowances should do so in consultation with a physician and/or qualified nutritionist.

Body Restoration

To be effective and enjoy life to the utmost, periodic recuperation is an essential ingredient in daily living patterns. Body restoration in the form of rest and sleep provide us with the means of revitalizing ourselves to meet the challenges of our responsibilities. In order to keep fatigue at a minimum and in its proper proportion in the cycle of everyday activities, nature has provided us with ways to help combat and reduce it. (The reader is asked to reflect back to the discussion of acute and chronic fatigue in Chapter 4.)

Activity is essential to life, but so are rest and sleep, as they afford the body the chance to regain its vitality and efficiency in a very positive way. Learning to utilize opportunities for rest and sleep may add years to our lives and zest to our years. Although rest and sleep are closely allied, they are not synonymous. For this reason it seems appropriate to consider them separately.

In general, most people think of *rest* as just "taking it easy." A chief purpose of rest is to reduce tension so that the body may be better able to recover from fatigue. There is no overt activity involved, but neither is there loss of consciousness as in sleep. In rest there is no loss of awareness of the external environment as in sleep. Since the need for sleep is usually in direct proportion to the type of activity in which we engage, it follows naturally that the more strenuous the activity, the more frequently the rest periods should be. A busy day may not be as noticably active as a game of tennis; nevertheless, it is the wise person who will let the body dictate when a rest period is required. Five or ten minutes of sitting in a chair with eyes closed may make the difference in the course of an active day. The real effectiveness of rest periods depends largely on the individual and his or her ability to let down and rest.

Sleep is a phenomenon that has never been clearly defined or understood but has aptly been named the "great restorer." An old Welsh proverb states that "disease and sleep are far apart." It is no wonder that authorities on the subject agree that sleep is essential to the vital functioning of the body and that natural sleep is the most satisfying form of recuperation from fatigue. It is during the hours of sleep that the body is given the opportunity to revitalize itself. All vital functions are slowed down so that the building of new cells, and the repair of tissues can take place without undue interruption. This does not mean that the body builds and regenerates tissue only during sleep, but it does mean that it is the time that nature has set aside to accomplish the task more easily. The body's metabolic rate is lowered, some waste products are eliminated, and energy is restored.

Throughout the ages many theories about sleep have been advanced. The ancient Greeks believed that sleep was the result of the blood supply to the brain being reduced. A later idea about sleep was based on the research conducted by the Russian scientist Ivan Pavlov. That is, that sleep was an aspect of the *conditioned reflex*. According to this theory the brain is "conditioned" to respond to any stimulus to become more active. And, the brain can develop the habit of reacting to certain stimuli with the slowing down of the activity. This means that when one is in an environment associated with sleep (bedroom) the brain gets a signal to start to slow down and finally one goes to sleep.

This theory was followed by one that suggested that while awake the body stored up waste products that tended to dull the higher centers of the brain, thus causing one to sleep.

In more modern times scientists are of the opinion that sleep occurs in cycles and each of these cycles, which are 1½ to 2 hours in length, a sleeper uses about 75% of this time in what is called S sleep. This is concerned with what are referred to as Delta brain waves in which one is in deep sleep. The second stage is known as D sleep. At this time one may be in deep sleep but at the same time some parts of the nervous system are active and there are *rapid eye movements* (REM). The theory is that S sleep restores the body physically and D sleep restores it psychically.

Despite the acknowledged need for sleep, a question of paramount importance concerns the amount of sleep necessary for the body to accomplish its recuperative task. There is no clear-cut answer to this query. Sleep is an individual matter based on degree rather than kind. The usual recommendation for adults is eight hours of sleep out of every 24, but the basis for this could well be fallacy rather than fact. There are many persons who can function effectively on much less sleep while others require more. No matter how many hours of sleep one gets during the course of a 24-hour period the real test of adequacy will depend largely upon how one feels. If you are normally alert, feel healthy, and are in good humor, you are probably getting a sufficient amount of sleep. The rest that sleep normally brings to the body depends to a large extent upon a person's freedom from excessive emotional tension and ability to relax. Unrelaxed sleep has little restorative value, but learning to relax is a skill that is not acquired in one night. (Some recommendations in this connection will be made in Chapter 7.)

Is loss of sleep dangerous? This is a question that is pondered quite frequently. Again, the answer is not simple. To the normally healthy person with normal sleep habits an occasional missing of the accustomed hours of sleep is not serious. On the other hand, repeated loss of sleep over a period of time can be dangerous. It is the loss of sleep night after night rather than at one time that apparently does the damage and results in the condition previously described as chronic fatigue. The general effects of loss of sleep are likely to result in poor general health, nervousness, irritability, inability to concentrate, lowered perseverance of effort, and serious fatigue. Under normal conditions a night of lost sleep followed by a period of prolonged sleep will restore the individual to his normal physiological self. Incidentally, the older adults in my surveys indicated that on average they received about 7½ hours of sleep each night. Remember this is an average and there were various deviations from this.

There are many conditions that tend to rob the body of restful slumber. Mental anguish and worry play a large part in holding sleep at bay.

Other factors that influence the quality of sleep are hunger, cold, boredom, and excessive fatigue. However, in many instances these factors can be kept under control.

In my interviews with older adults some complained of not being able to get a good night's sleep. Upon questioning it appeared that there were three more or less general reasons for this: (1) Most of them were far too inactive during the day and as a consequence were not tired when it came time to go to bed, (2) In some cases several of them tended to take prolonged naps during the day, resulting in their staying awake during the night, and (3) Some had recently moved into their present new environment and were having a rather difficult time adjusting to the new regimen and routine.

Many recommendations about sleep have been made by various sources some of which can be summarized as follows:

1. Relax physically and mentally before retiring.
2. Reduce your tension level during the day.
3. Manage your time, activities, and thoughts to prepare for a good night's sleep.
4. The process should be the same each night, and should begin at the same hour, leading to repose at the same hour.
5. Avoid stimulants before retiring; however, for some people a glass of warm milk can help one to become restful.

Understanding the complex nature of sleep may be the province of scientists and other qualified experts, but an understanding of the value of sleep is the responsibility of everyone.

HOW SOME OLDER ADULTS ARE MANAGING STRESS

One dimension of my surveys of stress among older adults was concerned with what measures they were taking in dealing with stress. This information is summarized in the following discussion.

One rather disturbing statistic revealed that about one third of the respondents indicated that they were more or less at a loss on how to deal with stress. A common response was to "grin and bear it" and many in this classification felt that it caused more stress. Many others said they "tried to forget" but that this did not help.

Almost four-fifths of the respondents used *recreational activities* as a coping measure, with about half of these citing reading as the favorite activity.

Slightly over 70% used *physical exercise* as a method of coping, the most popular activity being walking with well over two-thirds engaging in this form of exercise. On questioning, however, walking was in the nature of "strolling" and not "brisk" walking that will be described in the following chapter. A large proportion of the respondents professed a need for more knowledge about exercise. This third side of the fitness triangle will be dealt with in detail in the following chapter.

While about one-half of the respondents said that they engaged in the use of alcohol for "social drinking" purposes, slightly over one-fourth said they used an alcoholic beverage to relieve stress. As one 83-year-old man put it, "When I feel stressed I take a drink which relaxes me." Although this practice should not necessarily be condemned, at the same time it seems appropriate to cite exerpts from a recent report on older adults and the use of alcoholic beverages.[46]

Drinking patterns among older adults are studied by the National Institute on Alcohol Abuse and Alcoholism (NIAAA). There are two groups of older "problem drinkers"—defined by the NIAAA as anyone who drinks enough to interfere with physical and social functioning. The largest group consists of people who have been drinking heavily all their lives and have managed somehow to survive into late life. But a growing number are found in the second group: those who increased their consumption after age 60. In fact, a 1988 Mayo Clinic study found that 41% of persons age 65 and older enrolled in the Clinic's alcoholism program first reported symptoms of alcoholism after age 60.

According to Dr. Gene Cohen, Director of the National Institute on Aging, it is difficult to pinpoint the motives for some late-life drinkers. Although no one knows for sure why some persons start to drink for the first time it is speculated that some retirees may drink to relieve boredom. In addition, many retirees currently have more time than those in past years and thus this may lead to more social drinking.

It is interesting to note that the rise in late-life drinking coincides with the trend toward earlier retirement, leading some to believe that unexpected pressures (stress) stemming from this change may trigger a drinking habit. Older men make up most of the number of elderly alcoholics, although the number of older women who drink heavily in late life is starting to rise. And, finally, studies show that older adults are at the highest risk of becoming alcohol abusers after losing a spouse through death, divorce or legal separation. Because women live longer than men, they are more likely to find themselves isolated in later years.

Only about six percent said they used tranquilizers for the purpose of relieving stress and these were about equally divided between prescription and non-prescription drugs.

Slightly over 10% engaged in meditation as a stress-reducing technique. All of these respondents reported great success with the technique and recommended it for everyone. In other populations that I have studied only about five percent use meditation. One exception to this is psychiatrists with 20% of them using the technique.

Slightly more than 40% said they tried to use some sort of muscle relaxation to reduce stress and many of these were members of retirement residences where this activity was a part of an organized stress management program. This was also true of the practice of meditation. Later chapters will go into both of these techniques in detail.

Finally, slightly over one-half said they were able to reduce stress by resorting to divine guidance such as praying and reading the Bible. Almost 90% of these were women.

In this general regard a study by Ross[47] is of interest. Using a representative sample of 401 18–83 year old Illinois residents and controlling for sociodemographics and willingness to express feelings, her telephone survey found that the stronger a person's religious belief, the lower the level of psychological distress. This supported the idea that religion reduces demoralization and provides hope and meaning. However, a very interesting finding was that persons with no religion also had low levels of distress. Protestants had the lowest distress levels, followed by Catholics, Jews, and others. Difference in belief systems, however, especially a belief in the American Protestant ethic, did not explain differences in distress among religious groups.

This chapter has been concerned pretty much with general methods of dealing with stress. The final five chapters will take more specific stress coping techniques into account.

Chapter 6

STRESS, EXERCISE AND OLDER ADULTS

Physical *exercise* can be defined as engaging in body movement for the purpose of developing and maintaining physical fitness.

People of all ages tend to get much less exercise than they actually need. This is particularly true of older adults. In fact, it is estimated that much less than half of the population over 60 years of age engages in regular exercise. This may be due partly to what Ostrow and his associates[48] have identified as "age-grading." This means that early in life many people consider it inappropriate for older adults to engage in certain kinds of physical activity.

Ostrow also observed that many older individuals do not have accurate information about exercise that would enable them to exercise independently on their own. Ageism—prejudicial and discriminatory views about aging—is rampant in American society, and is especially pronounced in the context of exercise. In Fact, Conrad's[49] investigations of the attitudes of senior citizens toward activity showed that the elderly believe that the need for activity declines with age.

Dr. Bonnie G. Berger,[50] a distinguished sports psychologist and member of my board of reviewers for *Human Stress: Current Selected Research* contends that in addition to the age-grading of exercise, two fallacies contribute to the low percentage of older adults who are regular exercisers. The fallacies promoted by the age stratification of exercise activities need to be dispelled through educational programs before many elderly will consider a vigorous exercise program. She suggests that these fallacies that prevent more extensive exercise participation by the elderly include the beliefs that: (1) a person needs less exercise as he or she ages (i. e., exercise is primarily for children), and (2) exercise is hazardous to the health of many older adults either by (a) precipitating a heart attack, or elevating blood pressure, or by (b) exacerbating pre-existing medical conditions such as arthritis or Parkinson's disease.

Berger suggests one way to help elderly participants dispel such fallacies is to provide an exercise program that is initially closely supervised by a team of experts such as cardiologists, an exercise physiologist, and a sports psychologist. She and her associates have done this in an exercise study at Brooklyn College in which participants ranged in age from 65 to 80 years of age. Psychological and physiological responses were monitored closely throughout a 12 week program. The participants grew more confident about their physical abilities, reported mood enhancement, and improved on a variety of fitness indices. They also recognized their need for exercise as illustrated by their actual hiring of the exercise leader to continue the exercise program as a group activity upon completion of the study.

Unfortunately many older adults feel that they get enough exercise just by virtue of the fact that they are "moving around." Too many older adults adopt the concept that when they retire, that this is the time in life to "Just do nothing." But nothing could be further from the truth. It will be the intent of this chapter to dispel some of the false notions about exercise for older adults, as well as to discuss its benefits as a means of relief of stress and tension.

THE PHYSICAL ASPECT OF PERSONALITY

One point of departure in discussing the physical aspect of personality could be to state that "everybody has a body." Some are short, some are tall, some are lean, and some are fat. People come in different sizes, but all of them have a certain innate capacity that is influenced by the environment.

As far as human beings are concerned—from early childhood through older adulthood—it might be said that the body is our base of operation, what well could be called our "physical base." The other components of the total personality—social, emotional, and intellectual—are somewhat vague. Although these are manifested in various ways, we do not always see them as we do the physical aspect. Consequently, it becomes all important that starting as children a serious attempt be made to gain control over the physical aspect, or what is known as basic body control. The ability to do this of course will vary from one person to another. It will depend to a large extent upon our status of physical fitness.

The broad area of physical fitness can be broken down into certain components, and it is important that individuals achieve to the best of their natural ability as far as these components are concerned. There is not complete agreement as far as identification of the components of physical fitness are concerned. However, the following information provided some years ago by the President's Council on Physical Fitness and Sports[51] considers certain components to be basic:

1. **Muscular Strength.** This refers to the contraction power of muscles. The strength of muscles is usually measured with dynamometers or tensiometers, which record the amount of force particular muscle groups can apply in a single maximum effort. Man's existence and effectiveness depend upon his muscles. All movements of the body or any of its parts are impossible without action by muscles attached to the skeleton. Muscles perform vital functions of the body as well. The heart is a muscle; death occurs when it ceases to contract. Breathing, digestion, and elimination are dependent upon muscular contractions. These vital muscular functions are influenced by exercising the skeletal muscles; the heart beats faster, the blood circulates through the body at a greater rate, breathing comes deep and rapid, and perspiration breaks out on the surface of the skin.

2. **Muscular Endurance.** Muscular endurance is the ability of muscles to perform work. Two variations of muscular endurance are recognized: *isometric,* whereby a maximum static muscular contraction is held and *isotonic,* whereby the muscles continue to raise and lower a submaximal load as in weight training or performing push-ups. In the isometric form, the muscles maintain a fixed length; in the isotonic form, they alternatively shorten and lengthen. (These two forms of muscular endurance with regard to exercise will be discussed in detail later in the chapter.) Muscular endurance must assume some muscular strength. However, there are distinctions between the two; muscle groups of the same strength may possess different degrees of endurance.

3. **Circulatory-Respiratory Endurance.** Circulatory-respiratory endurance is characterized by moderate contractions of large muscle groups for relatively long periods of time, during which maximal adjustments of the circulatory-respiratory system to the activity are necessary, as in distance running and swimming. Obviously, strong and enduring muscles are needed. However, by themselves they are not enough; they do not guarantee well-developed circulatory-respiratory functions.

As far as the physical aspect of personality is concerned a major objective of modern man should be directed to maintaining a suitable level of physical fitness, the topic of the ensuing discussion.

MAINTAINING A SUITABLE LEVEL OF PHYSICAL FITNESS

Physical fitness presupposes an adequate intake of good food and an adequate amount of rest and sleep, but beyond these things, activity involving all the big muscles of the body is essential. Just how high a level of physical fitness should be maintained from one stage of life to another is a difficult question to answer because we must raise the following question: "Fitness for what?" Obviously, the young varsity athlete needs to think of a level of fitness far above that which will concern the average older adult.

Physical fitness has been described in different ways by different people; however, when all of these descriptions are put together it is likely that they will be characterized more by their similarities than by their differences. For purposes here I will think of physical fitness as the level of ability of the human organism to perform certain physical tasks or, put another way, the fitness to perform various specified tasks requiring muscular effort.

A reasonable question to raise at this point is: "Why is a reasonably high level of physical fitness desirable in modern times when there are so many effort-saving devices available that, for many people, strenuous activity is really not necessary anymore?" One possible answer to this is that all of us stand at the end of a long line of ancestors, all of whom at least lived long enough to have children because they were fit and vigorous, strong enough to survive in the face of savage beasts and savage men, and able to work hard. Only the fit survived. As a matter of fact, not very far back in your family tree, you would find people who had to be rugged and extremely active in order to live. Vigorous action and physical ruggedness are our biological heritage. Possibly because of the kind of background that we have, our bodies simply function better when we are active.

The word *exercise* may tend to have strong moralistic overtones. Like so many things that are said to "be good for you," it also tends to give rise to certain feelings of boredom and resentment. Thus, many people draw more than facetious pleasure in repeating the old sayings: "When I feel like exercising, I lie down quickly until the feeling goes away," and "I get my exercise serving as pall-bearer for my friends who exercised."

Most child development specialists agree that vigorous play in childhood is essential for the satisfactory growth of the various organs and systems of the body. It has been said that "play is the business of childhood." To conduct this "business" successfully and happily, the child should be physically fit. Good nutrition, rest, and properly conducted physical activities in and out of school can do much to develop and maintain the physical fitness of children and youth. Continuing this practice throughout life should be an essential goal of all mankind — including of course older adults!

EXERCISE AND THE AGING PROCESS

Dr. Kenneth Cooper, famous for his work in the area of aerobics, likes to say in his lectures that "aging slows running, but running slows aging." And, of course it is true. A point that should be made clear, however, is that nothing will *stop* or *reverse* the aging process, but it has been clearly demonstrated that exercise will *slow it down*. In addition, it has been shown that exercise can *prolong* life. For example, an 8-year study at Kenneth Cooper's Institute of Aerobic Research indicated that healthy men who do not exercise have a 3.44 times greater chance of dying from all causes when compared to those who work out vigorously. Also, sedentary women have a 4.15 times greater chance of dying from all causes when compared to the most fit women.

If I may be permitted to get a little technical I can explain the phenomenon of how exercise can slow down the aging process.

Everyone's body has the ability to take up and deliver oxygen to the working muscles. "Taking up" means that the oxygen in the lungs is taken up by the blood and "delivered" means that the oxygen is transported to the working muscles. The formula for this is VO_2max.

At about age 25, VO_2 max begins to decrease at about the rate of 8% per decade. This is for the sedentary person. Now, if one were to exercise moderately for three days per week for 20–30 minutes at 70% capacity this rate will be cut to about one half or about 4%. And this is the basis for how exercise can slow down the aging process.

An explanation of 70% capacity needs to be made. This is in terms of what is called the "target heart training range" (TR). This means that the range of intensity (heart beats per minute) is the extent to which levels of fitness can be improved without overworking or straining the body. When exercising, one is working beyond the resting state. The ordinary recommendation is not to elevate this rate over 80 or 85%. Older adults need to be careful not to push too hard and a good fitness level can be obtained with 60–70%. A rule of thumb method of determining your maximum heart rate is to subtract your age from 220. As an example the maximum heart rate for the average 70 year old would be 150. Seventy percent of this would be a rate of 105 beats per minute. The training level for 60% would be 90. A more accurate rate can be determined by a stress test conducted under the supervision of a cardiologist and this is recommended for older adults in pursuing an exercise program.

Regular exercise can have a positive affect on an older adult's general health and there is a strong likelihood that it will help to increase longevity. Older adults who feel young and seem young to others are ordinarily those who have continued to live active lives in their later years.

THEORIES OF HOW EXERCISE REDUCES STRESS

The value of exercise as a means of reducing stress is well documented by various sources. The previously-mentioned Bonnie G. Berger[52] suggests that because of its psychological and physiological benefits, exercise is an ideal stress reduction technique for older adults. It is accompanied by reductions in anxiety, depression, and anger—three common psychological stress symptoms. Exercise also improves several other psychological stress symptoms by enhancing the participants' vigor and clear-mindedness. In addition, regular exercise reduces several physical stress symptoms such as elevated heart rate, blood pressure, obesity, and general muscular tension. Finally, she points out its specific advantages when it is compared to other stress reduction techniques. In contrast to biofeedback, it requires no complicated equipment. The side effects of drugs are avoided, and a variety of physical benefits accrue: weight reduction, improved appearance, and increased energy and cardiovascular endurance.

According to Walter McQuade and Ann Aikman,[53] one of the many stresses people suffer from is stress resulting from their own pent-up aggressive drives. When people express these drives in physical action, they are better off because exercise not only dispels this form of stress, but also it enables the body to hold up better against stress in general.

Beata Jencks[54] theorizes that physical and emotional trauma upset balance of body and mind, and that much energy is wasted in muscular tension, bringing on unnecessary tiredness and exhaustion. If stress reactions become habit patterns, then the muscles and tendons shorten and thicken and excessive connective tissue is deposited, causing a general consolidation of tissues. She comments further that excess energy, released by action of the sympathetic nervous system, if not immediately dissipated by muscular action, produces muscular or nervous system tension and that this tension should be dissipated by muscular action in the form of exercise.

It has been suggested by C. Eugene Walker,[11] of the University of Oklahoma Medical School and one of my associates on a stress project that exercise is very effective in reducing anxiety, although he states that how this occurs is not entirely understood. It may be that it satisfies the evolutionary need of man to engage in large muscle, physically aggressive activity that was very adaptive for primitive man, but with our highly civilized sedentary, and confined lifestyle, has fewer acceptable outlets. He concludes that whatever the basis for it, exercise does have an anxiety- and tension-reducing effect. People on exercise programs tend to be more healthy, have better vital capacity, handle problems better, sleep better, and cope with life in general in a more satisfactory way. Over a period of time people on such programs generally feel better, are more optimistic, and have better self images. Thus, exercise immediately reduces anxiety somewhat and over the long run tends to inoculate against the development of future anxieties.

BENEFITS OF EXERCISE FOR OLDER ADULTS

As an "old gym teacher" and recent octogenarian who has exercised regularly throughout life, I can summarize my feelings about exercising and maintaining some level of physical fitness by saying that doing so makes possible types of meaningful experiences in life that are not otherwise available to you. These experiences include all manner of physical activity and exercise, and they also include the rich and satisfying interpersonal relationships that are usually associated with these activities. But maintaining some level of physical fitness has still another value that is usually not fully appreciated. This value has to do with the idea that the entire personality of every individual rests upon, and is dependent upon, its physical base. The entire personality—which is to say, all of the intellectual, emotional, and social components—is threatened when the physical component, the base of operation, is weak or unreliable. It has been claimed by fitness enthusiasts that academic performance, emotional control, and social adjustments are improved when an adequate level of physical fitness is improved; and many case histories and clinical data would tend to support this contention. However, at the moment, I would contend that a reasonably solid physical base is more likely than a shaky one to serve you as a successful launching pad for other personality resources. In other words, you will be likely to do better in everything you undertake if you feel good, your vitality is high, and you are capable of prolonged effort. These statements can be backed up by authoritative opinion and research, some of which is included in the following discussion.

Having spent several years researching in the area of exercise and aging,[55] R. J. Shepard summarized the findings as follows: A well-designed training program not only increases life satisfaction, but also augments maximum oxygen intake by at least 20%, with associated increases of muscle strength and joint flexibility, dispersal of accumulated fat, and halting of bone mineral loss. The subsequent rate of aging is unchanged, but it takes many more years to reach the situation where working capacity is insufficient to meet the demands of either occupation or personal care.

In his outstanding book, *Longevity: Fulfilling Our Biological Potential,* Kenneth Pelletier[56] identified five characteristics that are common in centenarian communities throughout the world such as those in the Ecuadorian Andes, and the Caucasus Mountains in what was previously the Soviet Union. People in such areas live abnormally long lives and one of the characteristics of this identified by Pelletier was exercise. He expressed it as follows: Physical activity is . . . perhaps most important as a factor in the longevity and optimum health exhibited in these centerarian communities.

The fact that exercise can improve the *cognitive abilities* of older adults is shown in a study by Clarkson-Smith and Hartley.[57] The subjects were 62 men and women ages 55–88 who exercised vigorously and 62 sedentary individuals in the same age range. Variables such as education and medical condition were taken into consideration. The experimental group performed significantly better on measures of reasoning, working memory and reaction time—all of which reflect brain functions. The authors concluded that exercise may help to forestall degenerative changes in the brain associated with normal aging.

Some older adults suffering from *depression* have benefited from exercise and two studies are reported here.

In a study of older adults between the ages of 60 and 80 years, Uson and Larrosa[58] reported that 70% of those who exercised for an hour twice a week for nine months showed reductions in depression as measured by

Zung's Depression Inventory Scale. In contrast, 40% of age-matched individuals who belonged to clubs for retired persons showed increases in depression. No explanation for the increase in depression was given other than it was "a fact which gives an idea of the rapid deterioration of these persons." The supervised exercise program included warm-ups, flexibility and abdominal strength exercises, and a slowly paced 10-minute run. Exercisers also improved on measures of neuroticism and reported decreases in the number of psychomatic complaints and doctor visits.

In the second study of exercise and depression, Bennett, Carmack and Gardner[59] evaluated the effects of exercise on 38 elderly nursing home residents and senior community center participants. Subjects were three males and 35 females between the ages of 50 and 98 years. The program lasted for eight weeks with two 45 minute sessions per week. The program included only balance and flexibility activities. Exercisers who showed signs of clinical depression as measured by the Zung Self-Rating Depression Scale reported significantly less depression at the end of the eight-week exercise sessions.

Many older adults complain of "being stiff in the joints." This pertains to *flexibility* —range of motion in a joint. Some of the research on flexibility in older adults and exercise is reported here.

One study by Frekany and Leslie[60] was conducted to see whether or not significant improvement in flexibility could be demonstrated by older adults who participated in a fitness program. Fifteen women from ages 71–90 exercised for 30 minutes twice weekly for about seven months. There was significant improvement for ankle flexion and lower back flexion.

In another study Bassett, McClamrock and Schmelzer[61] examined the effects of exercise on flexibility measures with a group of 18 people 60 years or older. They met three times a week for 30 minutes for a total of 29 sessions. Results showed significant improvement in the shoulder-hip-knee flexibility.

In a final study reported here by Chapman, deVries and Swezey[62] the effects of an exercise program on finger joint resistance (stiffness) among 20 older men 63 to 88 years, and 20 males 15 to 18 were examined. The right index finger was exercised by lifting weights attached to a pulley for a total of 18 sessions over six weeks. In the beginning the older men had significantly greater joint stiffness than the younger men, although the older men had the same significant improvements in flexibility as the younger men. This study demonstrated that joint stiffness is also reversible, and young and old reacted in the same manner to the training.

Sometimes *self-esteem* decreases in older adults due to a variety of factors. For instance, lower self-esteem can be generated by negative attitudes that some younger people have toward older adults. Other factors are concerned with a decline in social interaction and the power and control some older adults have over their environment. Situations that place a value on abilities of older adults, as well as to respect their right to make decisions go a long way in increasing self-esteem. There has been some research in this area and one representative example is reported here. Perri and Templer[63] had 23 persons in the 60–69 year age range participate in an aerobic exercise program. There was a control group of 19 persons ranging from 60–78 years of age. Those in the experimental group exercised three times weekly for 14 weeks while the control group continued their normal lifestyle. The study revealed significant increases in self-concept for the experimental group.

It seems appropriate to close this section of the chapter by giving some of the comments of Walter Bortz, M.D., former president of the American Geriatric Society and cochairman of the American Medical Association's Committee on Aging:[64]

- Aging may result more from lack of exercise than from the number of years one can count on the calendar.
- A great deal of what passes for change due to age is not really that at all, but rather the result of inactivity.
- Exercise is now listed as valuable for numerous medical conditions, including coronary heart disease, hypertension, obesity, diabetes, osteoporosis, and depression.
- Dr. Bortz concludes that: "No single medical prescription bears such an impressive list of benefits as does exercise. Until recently a physician who prescribed exercise for a patient was labeled a kook. In the near future, a physician who doesn't prescribe exercise under certain circumstances will be guilty of malpractice."

TYPES OF EXERCISE

In general, there are three types of exercises: (1) *Proprioceptive-facilitative*, (2) *isotonic*, and (3) *isometric* (in reading this section of the chapter the reader is asked to reflect back to the discussion of the components of physical fitness—muscular strength, muscular endurance, and circulatory-respiratory endurance).

Proprioceptive-Facilitative Exercises

These exercises are those that consist of various refined patterns of movement. Important in the performance of these exercises are those factors involved in movement: (1) time, (2) force, (3) space, and (4) flow.

Time is concerned with how long it takes to complete a movement. For example, a movement can be slow and deliberate, or a movement might be made with sudden quickness.

Force needs to be applied to set the body or one of its segments in motion and to change its speed and/or direction. Thus, force is concerned with how much strength is required for movement. Swinging the arms requires less strength than attempting to propel the body over the surface area with a standing broad jump.

In general, there are two factors concerned with *space.* These are the amount of space required to perform a particular movement and the utilization of available space.

All movements involve some degree of rhythm in their performance. Thus, *flow* is the sequence of movements involving rhythmic motion.

The above factors are included in all body movements in various degree. The degree to which each is used effectively in combination will determine the extent to which the movement is performed with skill. This is a basic essential in the performance of proprioceptive-facilitative exercises. In addition, various combinations of the following features are involved in the performance of this type of exercise.

1. **Muscular Power.** Ability to release maximum muscular force in the shortest time. Example: standing broad jump.

2. **Agility.** Speed in changing body position or in changing direction. Example: Dodging run.

3. **Speed.** Rapidity with which successive movements of the same kind can be performed. Example: Speed running.

4. **Flexibility.** Range of movement in a joint or a sequence of joints. Example: Touch floor with fingers without bending knees.

5. **Balance.** Ability to maintain position and equilibrium both in movement (dynamic balance) and while stationary (static balance). Examples: Walking on a line (dynamic); standing on one foot (static).

6. **Coordination.** Working together of the muscles and organs of the

human body in the performance of a specific task. Example: Throwing or catching an object.

Several of the respondents in my surveys engaged in such proprioceptive-facilitative activities as tennis, raquetball, handball, squash and volleyball. However, this occurred most often when they either belonged to a sports club or in retirement residences where facilities and instruction were available for such purposes.

Isotonic Exercises

An isotonic exercise involves the amount of resistance one can overcome during one application of force through the full range of motion in a given joint or joints. An example of this would be picking up a weight and flexing the elbows while lifting the weight to shoulder height.

Isotonics can improve strength to some extent. They are also very useful for increasing and maintaining full range of motion. Such range of motion should be maintained throughout life if possible although it can decrease with age and with such musculoskeletal disorders as arthritis. This disease can cause shortening of fibrous tissue structures and this is likely to limit the normal range of motion.

Another important feature of isotonic exercise is that it can increase circulatory-respiratory endurance in activities that use oxygen for prolonged periods. These activities are referred to as *aerobics* and include running, walking and swimming. The term aerobics derives from the Greek work *aēr* which means "air." Aerobics will strengthen the lungs, heart, and cardiovascular system as a whole. Indeed any activity that causes one to "puff" hard enough could be classified as aerobic. For example, spirited folk and square dancing can help to accomplish this. Walking is an activity that is a favorite aerobic exercise of many older adults. But, it must be done correctly. It is important that one does *brisk* walking (some refer to it as *fast* walking) to derive the most benefit.

The reader may recall that a good proportion of the older adults in my surveys indicated that they exercised by walking. However, this was more in the nature of strolling and not the brisk type of walking just referred to.

In recent years there has been a tendency to compare walking with running as a fitness exercise. In this regard it has been shown that running a mile in 8½ minutes will use up about 26 more calories than doing a mile walk in 12 minutes. Also the walking pace is important. For example, the average walking rate is about three miles per hour. If this rate is increased by 25% we get into the category of "fitness walking." This means that by increasing the rate from three miles per hour to five miles per hour about twice as many calories are used up. At three miles an hour about 66 calories are burned per mile while at a five miles an hour pace about 124 calories are used up.

Brisk walking for older adults has much to commend it: (1) No equipment is necessary but good comfortable walking shoes are important, (2) It does not require other persons as participants although it can be pleasant to walk along with someone, and (3) It can be done just about anywhere there is a suitable surface area available.

Walking is a fine exercise for improving circulatory-respiratory endurance and many older adults find that a 20-minute brisk walk is invigorating and enjoyable. In fact, Pocari and associates[65] found that 91% of the women and 83% of the men age 50 or older reached a training heart rate (70% of maximal heart rate) when they walked a mile as fast as possible. You might want to check your pulse rate while walking to find out how much your heart rate is accelerating and the extent to which you are exercising up to capacity that you have established for yourself. (Refer back to the discussion on target heart training rate.)

If you decide that walking is the most suitable exercise for you, do so briskly: shoulders back, head up, come down on heels and walk through toes, swing arms and breathe deeply. Some older adults have found that a combination of walking *and* running is preferred. That is, as in the old Boy Scout Pace of 50 paces running and 50 paces walking.

Isometric Exercises

Although isometrics do not provide much in the way of improvement of normal range of motion and endurance, they are most useful in increasing strength and volume of muscles. In isometrics, the muscle is contracted, but the length of the muscle is generally the same during contraction as during relaxation. The contraction is accomplished by keeping two joints rigid while at the same time contracting the muscles(s) between the joints. A maximal amount of force is applied against a fixed resistance during one all-out effort. An example of this is pushing or pulling against an immovable object. Let us say that if you place your hands against a wall and push with as much force as you can, you have effected the contraction of certain muscles while their length has remained the same.

Using Isometrics in Stressful Situations

Many environments produce various kinds of stressful conditions. The present discussion is concerned with one's active behavior in a stressful situation. More specifically, what can one do in the way of physical activity to deal with a stressful situation in the immediate environment?

Various authentic pronouncements have been made that support the idea that instant activity can be beneficial. For example, Gal and Lazarus[66] report that being engaged in activity — rather than remaining passive — is preferable in most individuals in most stressful situations and can be highly effective in reducing threat and distress. Lazarus[67] has also maintained that a person may alter his or her psychological and physiological stress reactions in a given situation simply by taking action, and this in turn, will affect his or her appraisal of the situation thereby ultimately altering the stress reaction.

What then are some of the physical activities that one can engage in as a reaction to a stressful situation? Obviously, it would not be appropriate to engage in isotonics by dropping to the floor and start doing push-ups or to break into a two-mile jog around the room. Isometrics are recommended for this purpose and they can be performed in a more or less subtle manner and not necessarily be noticed by others. The following are some possibilities that I have developed and certainly creative individuals will be able to think of others.

1. **Hand and Head Press.** Interweave fingers and place hands at the back of the head with elbows pointing out. Push the head backward on the hands while simultaneously pulling the head forward with the hands. Although this can be done while standing, it can also be done while sitting at a desk or table and is less conspicious.

2. **Wall Press.** Stand with the back against the wall. Allow the arms to hang down at the sides. Turn hands toward the wall and press the wall with the palms, keeping the arms straight.

3. **Hand Pull.** Bend the right elbow and bring the right hand in with the palm up close to the front of the body. Put the left hand in the right hand. Try to curl the right arm upward while simultaneously resisting with the left hand. Repeat using the opposite pressure. This can be done while standing or sitting at a desk or table.

4. **Hand Push.** The hands are clasped with the palms together close to the chest with the elbows pointing out. Press the hands together firmly.

5. **Leg Press.** While sitting at a desk or table, cross the left ankle over the right ankle. The feet are on the floor and the legs are at about a right angle. Try to straighten the right leg while resisting with the left leg. Repeat with the right ankle over the left ankle.

6. **The Gripper.** Place one hand on the other and grip hard. Another variation is to grip an object. While standing, this could be the back of a chair or, while sitting, it could be the arms of a chair or the seat.

7. **Chair Push.** While sitting at a desk or table with the hand on the armrests of the chair, push down with the hands. The entire buttocks can be raised from the chair seat. One or both feet can be lifted off the floor, or both can remain in contact with the floor.

8. **Hip Lifter.** While sitting at a desk or table, lift one buttock after the other from the chair seat. Try to keep the head from moving. The hands can be placed at the sides of the chair seat for balance.

The isometric exercises recommended here have met with success with older adults who have practiced them in particular environments. You might wish to experiment with those that can be performed from a sitting position. It could be something to think about when your bridge partner is putting you under stress by a stupid play.

There is no set order for doing isometric exercises—nor does a whole series have to be completed at one time. For each contraction, maintain tension for no more than eight seconds—and less if it is more comfortable for you. (*NOTE:* It is possible that isometrics may be contraindicated for persons with hypertension; therefore persons with this condition might wish to consult their physician before proceeding.)

PLANNING YOUR OWN PROGRAM

In recommending physical activity—vigorous pleasurable physical activity—to older adults, I am doing so not only in the sense that it will be likely to reduce, eliminate, or avoid chronic fatigue and lessen the impact of acute fatigue. I recommend it, too, on the basis that the ability to move the body skillfully in a wide variety of ways and for appreciable periods of time is a dimension of human experience that is fundamental, pleasurable, and meaningful. It is part of being human and alive. To deprive ourselves of this category of living is as silly as closing the door to music, art, and good books. Man in motion is man alive!

The traditional recommendation has been to consult a physician before undertaking a physical activity program. It is likely that a physician will recommend the program without restriction, or if a physical problem is found, he will take steps to make it more suitable to you as an individual. If your personal physician is not well informed about exercise, ask him to recommend someone who is. One of the most important factors at the outset is to have a treadmill stress test under the supervision of a cardiologist.

The next consideration is that a program be an individual matter and one that fits your own needs and wishes. In other words, if a person is not happy with the program, it will be unlikely that it will meet with success as far as personal goals are concerned. Each individual will have to determine which particular approach is best for him or her, specified physical exercises, recreational sports, or a combination of both.

Three important factors to consider when formulating an exercise program for yourself are *frequency, persistence* and *adherence* and *positive reinforcement.*

Once you have decided what you are going to do for your exercise program, whether prescribed exercises or recreational sports (proprioceptive-facilitative exercises), you will need to determine how many times a week to engage in these activities. It is best to avoid extremes of the "once in a while" or "always without fail" spurts and try to maintain a regular schedule of three to four times a week. It is also a good idea to work out on alternate days—Monday, Wednesday, and Friday, or Tuesday, Thursday and Saturday. Sunday can be used as a makeup day. The hour of the day does not necessarily matter. However, it should be remembered if you have already decided that your fitness program is going to be high on your priority list of things to do, it should not be difficult to get into the habit of putting regular workouts into your weekly schedule.

Persistence and adherence are as important to any exercise program as the activities or exercises themselves. You will obtain much better and more lasting results from a program of three or four steady and regular workouts each week than a program where you go all out every day for one week and then do nothing at all the following two or three weeks. Once you commit yourself to your program, stick with it and do not let anything interfere with it. Your maintenance program, once you have reached your desired level of fitness, might be less strenuous and/or slightly less frequent, but you will lose whatever results you have built up or gained if your activity program ceases completely or becomes too sporadic.

Psychological research has discovered that a response that is reinforced by some means is more apt to be repeated than one that is not. When this kind of research was first studied, it was thought that the reward of desired behavior and the punishment of undesired behavior created equal and opposite effects. It was quickly discovered that this was not the case. Punishment seems to have a less permanent effect than reward, and punishment may even bring about the opposite results from the intended one. Therefore, it is positive reinforcement that we are seeking. Although there seems to be plenty of positive reinforcement built right into your fitness program (looking and feeling better), you will also need to be reassured that you will be receiving praise and encouragement from the people around you as you get started and continue in your fitness program. This also works both ways. If some members of your family or someone you know is attempting to change his or her fitness condition, by all means offer encouragement and praise. Make them feel good about what they are doing or trying to do. Obviously, it should go without saying that criticizing or belittling are the easiest ways to put a damper on, or even wipe out completely, a person's confidence in himself and his enthusiasm for his program.

Chapter 7

RELAXATION CAN REDUCE STRESS

R ELAX!!! How many times have you heard this expression? Although it has frequent usage as a means of telling a person to "take it easy," or "slow down," more often than not those using the expression are not aware of its real meaning. This was the case with the older adults in my surveys. It may be recalled that about 40% of them said they used muscle relaxation to reduce stress. However, upon questioning, many of these individuals were confused as to the difference between "resting" the muscles and "relaxing" them. Thus the need for a better understanding of deep muscle relaxation.

Most of us need some form of relaxation in order to relieve the tensions encountered in daily living. The purpose of this chapter is to explore various facets of relaxation, along with those kinds of conditions that tend to produce a relaxed state. There are many procedures that can help improve a person's ability to relax, and thus reduce stress. It should be borne in mind that what may be satisfactory for one person may not necessarily be so for another.

THE MEANING OF RELAXATION

The reality of muscle fibers is that they have a response repertoire of one. All they can do is contract and this is the response they make to the electrochemical stimulation of impulses via the motor nerves. *Relaxation is the removal of this stimulation.*[68]

A few years ago Dr. Herbert Benson[69] introduced the term, *relaxation response*. This involves a number of bodily changes that occur in the organism when one experiences deep muscle relaxation. There is a response against "overstress," which brings on these bodily changes and brings the body back into what is a healthier balance. Thus, the purpose of any kind of relaxation technique should be to induce a relaxation response.

I need to interject here that the following two chapters will take into account the stress reduction techniques of *meditation* and *biofeedback*, both of which can indeed be considered as relaxation techniques. Therefore, it seems important at this point that attention be given to the theory underlying these techniques, all of which are concerned with mind-body interactions, and all of which are designed to induce the relaxation response. In *progressive relaxation*, it is theorized that if the muscles of the body are relaxed, the mind in turn will be quiet. The theory involved in *meditation* is that if the mind is quieted, then other systems of the body will tend to be more readily stabilized. In the practice of *biofeedback*, the theoretical basis tends to involve some sort of integration of progressive relaxation and meditation. It is believed that the brain has the potential for voluntary control over all the systems it monitors, and is affected by all of these systems. Thus, it is the intimacy of interaction between mind and body that has provided the mechanism through which one can learn voluntary control over biological activity.[70]

From the point of view of the physiologist, relaxation is sometimes considered as "zero activity," or as nearly zero as one can manage in the neuromuscular system. That is, it is a neruomuscular accomplishment that results in reduction, or possible complete absence of muscle tone in a part of, or in the entire body. It has been suggested that a primary value of relaxation lies in the lowering of brain and spinal cord activity, resulting from a reduction of nerve impulses arising in muscle spindles and other sense endings in muscles, tendons, and joint structures.

The terms *relaxation* and *refreshment* are sometimes confused in their meaning. While these factors are important to the well-being of the human organism, they should not be used interchangeably to mean the same thing. *Refreshment* is the result of an improved blood supply to the brain for "refreshment" from central fatigue and to the muscles for the disposition of their waste products. This explains in part why mild muscular activity is good for overcoming the fatigue of sitting quietly (seventh inning stretch) and for hastening recovery after strenuous exercise (an athlete continuing running for a short distance slowly after a race).[71]

For many years, recommendations have been made with regard to procedures individuals might apply in an effort to relax. Examples of some of these procedures are submitted in the ensuing discussions. In consideration of any technique designed to accomplish relaxation, one very important factor that needs to be taken into account is that learning to relax is a skill. That is, it is a skill based on the kinesthetic awareness of feelings of *tonus* (the normal degree of contraction present in most muscles, which keeps them always ready to function when needed). Unfortunately, it is a skill that very few of us practice—probably because we have little awareness of how to go about it.

One of the first steps in learning to relax is to experience tension. That is, one should be sensitive to tensions that exist in his or her body. This can be accomplished by voluntarily contracting a given muscle group, first very strongly and then less and less. Emphasis should be placed on detecting the signal of tension as the first step in "letting go"—(relaxing).

You might wish to try an experiment used to demonstrate this phenomenon. Raise one arm so that the palm of the hand is facing outward away from your face. Now, bend the wrist backward and try to point the fingers back toward your face and down toward the forearm. You should feel some *strain* at the wrist joint. You should also feel something else in the muscle and this is tension, which is due to the muscle contracting the hand backward. Now, flop the hand forward with the fingers pointing downward and you will have accomplished a *tension-relaxation* cycle.

As in the case of any muscular skill, learning how to relax takes time and one should not expect to achieve complete satisfaction immediately. After one has identified a relaxation technique that he or she feels comfortable with, increased practice should eventually achieve satisfactory results.

PROGRESSIVE RELAXATION

The technique of progressive relaxation was developed by Edmund Jacobson[72] many years ago. It is still the technique most often referred to in the literature and probably the one that has had the most widespread application. In this technique, the person concentrates on progressively relaxing one muscle group after another. The technique is based on the procedure of comparing the difference between tension and relaxation. That is, as previously mentioned, one senses the feeling of tension in order to get the feeling of relaxation. (*NOTE:* As in the case of isometrics, progressive relaxation could be contraindicated for persons with hypertension.)

As mentioned before, learning to relax is a skill that you can develop in applying the principles of progressive relaxation. One of the first steps is to be able to identify the various muscle groups and how to tense them so that tension and relaxation can be experienced. However, before making suggestions on how to tense and relax the various muscle groups, there are certain preliminary measures that need to be taken into account:

1. You must understand that this procedure takes time and like anything else, the more you practice the more proficient you should become with the skills.
2. Progressive relaxation is not the kind of thing to be done spontaneously, and you should be prepared to spend from 20 to 30 minutes daily in tensing-relaxing activities.
3. The particular time of day is important and this is pretty much an individual matter. Some recommendations suggest that progressive relaxation be practiced twice daily; sometime during the day and again in the evening before retiring.
4. It is important to find a suitable place to practice the tensing-relaxing activities. Again this is an individual matter with some preferring a bed or couch and others a comfortable chair.
5. Consideration should be given to the amount of time a given muscle is tensed. You should be sure that you are able to feel the difference between tension and relaxation. This means that tension should be maintained from about four to not more than eight seconds.
6. Another important point to take into account is what sort of "mental practice," if any, should be used as the muscles are tensed and relaxed. In this connection, some clinical psychologists may use mental practice predominantly, as in the case suggested later in the chapter.
7. Breathing is an important concomitant in tensing and relaxing muscles. To begin with, it is suggested that three or more deep breaths be taken and held for about five seconds. This will tend to make for better rhythm in breathing. Controlled breathing makes it easier to relax and it is most effective when it is done deeply and slowly. It is ordinarily recommended that one should inhale deeply when the muscles are tensed and exhale slowly when "letting go."

How To Tense and Relax Various Muscles

Muscle groups may be identified in different ways. The classification given here consists of four different groups: (1) muscles of the head, face, tongue, and neck; (2) muscles of the trunk; (3) muscles of the upper extremities; and (4) muscles of the lower extremities.

Muscles of the Head, Face, Tongue and Neck

There are two chief muscles of the head, the one covering the back of the head and the one covering the front of the skull. There are about 30 muscles of the face including muscles of the orbit and eyelids, mastication, lips, tongue, and neck. Incidentally, it has been estimated that it takes 26 facial muscles to frown and a proportionately much smaller number to smile.

Muscles of this group may be tensed and relaxed as follows (relaxation is accomplished by "letting go" after tensing):

1. Raise your eyebrows by opening the eyes as wide as possible. You might wish to look into a mirror to see if you have formed wrinkles on the forehead.
2. Tense the muscles on either side of your nose like you were going to sneeze.
3. Dilate or flare out your nostrils.
4. Force an extended smile from "ear to ear" at the same time clenching your teeth.
5. Pull one corner of your mouth up and the other up as in a "villainous sneer."
6. Draw your chin as close to your chest as possible.
7. Do the opposite of the above trying to draw your head back as close to your back as possible.

Muscles of the Trunk

Included in this group are the muscles of the back, chest, abdomen, and pelvis. Here are some ways you can tense some of these muscles.

1. Bring your chest forward and at the same time put your shoulders back with emphasis on bringing your shoulder blades as close together as possible.
2. Try to round your shoulders and bring your shoulders blades far apart. This is pretty much the opposite of the above.
3. Give your shoulders a shrug trying to bring them up to your ears at the same time as you try to bring your neck downward.
4. Breathe deeply and hold it momentarily and then blow out the air from your lungs rapidly.

5. Draw in your stomach so that your chest is out beyond your stomach. Exert your stomach muscles by forcing out to make it look like you are fatter in that area than you are.

Muscles of the Upper Extremities

This group includes muscles of the hands, forearms, upper arms, and shoulders. A number of muscles situated in the trunk may be grouped with the muscles of the upper extremities, their function being to attach the upper limbs to the trunk and move the shoulders and arms. In view of this there is some overlapping in muscle groups *two* and *three.* Following are some ways to tense some of these muscles.

1. Clench the fist and then open the hand, extending the fingers as far as possible.
2. Raise one arm shoulder high and parallel to the floor. Bend at the elbow and bring the hand in toward the shoulder. Try to touch your shoulders while attempting to move the shoulder away from your hand. Flex your opposite biceps in the same manner.
3. Stretch one arm to the side of the body and try to point the fingers backward toward the body. Do the same with the other arm.
4. Hold the arm out the same way as above but this time have the palm facing up and point the fingers inward toward the body. Do the same with the other arm.
5. Stretch one arm out to the side, clench the fist and roll the wrist around slowly. Do the same with the other arm.

Muscles of the Lower Extremeties

This group includes muscles of the hips, thighs, legs, feet, and buttocks. Following are ways to tense some of these muscles.

1. Hold one leg out straight and point your toes as far forward as you can. Do the same with the other leg.
2. Do the same as above but point your toes as far backward as you can.
3. Turn each foot outward as far as you can and release. Do just the opposite by turning the foot outward as far as you can.
4. Try to draw the thigh muscles up so that you can see the form of the muscles.
5. Make your buttocks tense by pushing down if you are sitting in a

chair. If you are lying down try to draw the muscles of the buttocks in close by attempting to force the cheeks together.

The above suggestions include several possibilities for tensing various muscles of the body. As you practice some of these, you will also discover other ways to tense and then let go. A word of caution might be that in the early stages, you should be alert to the possibility of cramping certain muscles. This can happen particularly with those muscles that are not frequently used. This means that at the beginning you should proceed carefully. It might be a good idea to keep a diary or record of your sessions so that you can refer back to these experiences if this might be necessary. This will also help you get into each new session by reviewing your experiences in previous sessions.

MENTAL PRACTICE AND IMAGERY IN RELAXATION

Mental practice is a symbolized rehearsal of a physical activity in the absence of any gross muscular movement. This means that a person imagines in his own mind the way he will perform a given activity. *Imagery* is concerned with the development of a mental image that may aid one in the performance of an activity. In mental practice, the person thinks through what he is going to do, and with imagery he may suggest to himself or another may suggest a condition to him, and he then tries to effect a mental image of the condition.

The use of mental practice in performing motor skills is not new. In fact, research in this general area has been going on for well over half a century. This research has revealed that imagining a movement will likely produce recordable electric action potentials emanating from the muscle groups that would be called up if the movement were to be actually carried out. In addition, most mental activity is accompanied by general rises in muscular tension.

One procedure in the use of mental practice for relaxation is that of making suggestions to one's self. For the most part, in early childhood, we first learn to act on the basis of verbal instructions from others. Later we learn to guide and direct our own behavior on the basis of our own language activities—we literally talk to ourselves, giving ourselves instructions. This point of view has long been supported by research that postulates that speech as a form of communication between children and adults later becomes a means of organizing the child's own behavior.

That is, the function that was previously divided between two people—child and adult—becomes an internal function of human behavior.

An example is an approach recommended by the previously-mentioned C. Eugene Walker[11] involving one making relaxation-connected statements to himself or herself. He suggests the following specific illustration:

I am going to relax completely. First, I will relax my forehead and scalp. I will let all the muscles of my forehead and scalp relax and become completely at rest. All of the wrinkles will come out of my forehead and that part of my body will relax completely. Now, I will relax the muscles of my face. I will just let them relax and go limp. There will be no tension in my jaw. Next, I will relax my neck muscles. Just let them become tranquil and allow all the pressure to leave them. My neck muscles are relaxing completely. Now, I will relax the muscles of my shoulders. That relaxation will spread down my arms to the elbows, down the forearms to the wrists, hands, and fingers. My arms will just dangle from the frame of my body. I will now relax the muscles of my chest. I will let them relax. I will take a deep breath and relax, letting all the tightness and tenseness leave. My breathing will now be normal and relaxed, and I will relax the muscles of my stomach. Now, I will relax all the muscles up and down both sides of the spine; now, the waist, buttocks, and thighs down to my knees. Now, the relaxation will spread to the calves of my legs, ankles, feet, and toes. I will just lie here and continue to let all the muscles go completely limp. I will become completely relaxed from the top of my head to the tips of my toes.

In what was termed the "release only" phase of relaxation training, Robert J. McBrien[73] used instructions involving imagery as follows:

Just imagine you are lying on your back on soft green grass . . . you are so comfortable as you look up through the branches and leaves of a shade tree at the deep blue sky . . . you can see soft white puffy clouds floating by (further instructions to focus on the pleasant feeling of relaxation would then follow).

Another way imagery can be used to promote a relaxed state is by making *comparative* statements such as "float like a feather," or "melt like ice." Creative persons (like yourself) will be able to think of many such comparative statements to assist in producing a relaxed state.

MAKING A GAME OF RELAXATION

A game format can be used as a means of providing satisfactory relaxation. Originally, this approach was used with children, but applying the philosophy that everyone is a "kid at heart," it has been applied successfully with adults of all ages. One advantage of this is that it can become more of a fun-oriented situation in case of boredom when using structured procedures. An example of the successful use of the game format is that which is suggested by the aforementioned Robert J. McBrien. He used this approach in the tensing and releasing phase with the game, *Simon Says.* Each muscle group to be tensed and then relaxed was prefaced by "Simon says: That is, Simon says to close your eyes ... Simon says to make your eyebrows touch your hair ... Simon says to let go and feel your eyes relax." A five-second tensing of any muscle was followed by 15 seconds of relaxing the muscle. The sequence for relaxing the muscles prefaced by "Simon says" was as follows:

1. Head
   a. Try to make your eyebrows touch your hair.
   b. Squeeze your eyes shut.
   c. Wrinkle your nose.
   d. Press your lips together.
   e. Press your tongue against the roof of your mouth.
2. Shoulders and Back
   a. Lift your shoulders and try to touch your ears.
   b. Bring your shoulders back as far as they will go.
3. Hands and Arms
   a. Make your fist as tight as you can.
   b. Show me your arm muscle.
4. Stomach
   a. Make your stomach as hard as you can; pull it way in.
5. Upper Legs
   a. Lift your legs and feet off the floor.
   b. Press your knees together.
6. Lower Legs and Feet
   a. Press your ankles together.
   b. Press your feet together against the floor.

(*Note:* On the unlikely possibility that the reader is not aware of it, the game *Simon says* is played as follows: One or more players face the person who plays Simon. Every time Simon says to do something, the players do it. However, if a command is given without the prefix "Simon says," the players remain motionless. For example, when the leader issues the command, "Simon says press your ankles together," everyone does this; but if the person playing Simon says, "Press your knees together," the players do not execute the command. The original purpose of this format was for use with children; however, experience has shown that it can be equally successful with adults.)

CREATIVE RELAXATION

There are at least two different versions of what can be termed *creative relaxation*. In his interesting book *High Level Wellness*, Donald B. Ardell[74] considers it to be an awakening of different parts of the breathing body, a gentle way of reaching the flow of vital energy deep within where experience and creativity penetrate each other. He further considers it as a movement meditation on the innate relationship between the breathing body and gravity; one means of harmonizing thought, feeling, and movement.

My own approach to creative relaxation was developed for the purpose of reducing stress in young children. However, it has gone far beyond this original purpose, since I have recently had successful applications of it with various older adult groups.

The creative relaxation approach, developed by the present author and his coauthor daughter, Joy N. Humphrey,[75] combines a form of imagery and tensing and releasing.

A person creates a movement(s) designed to tense and relax individual muscles, muscle-groups, or the entire body. The procedure is applicable in any kind of setting. It has been used with success in group settings in retirement residences.

Creative relaxation simply means that there are contrasting creative movements that give the effect of tensing and letting go. In a sense, it is somewhat like *Charades*. An illustration is provided here for a better understanding of the concept.

This example shows the contrast (tensing and letting go) of the muscles of an upper extremity (arm). The leader of a group could start by raising a question such as the following: "What would you say is the main difference between a ball bat and a jump rope?"

This question is then discussed and will no doubt lead to the major difference being that a ball bat is hard and stiff and that a jump rope is soft and limp. The group leader might then proceed as follows: "Let's see if we can all make one of our arms be like a ball bat." (This movement is created.) "Now, quickly, can you make your arm be like a jump rope?" (The movement is created by releasing the tensed arm.)

The experience can be evaluated by using these questions: "How did your arm feel when you made it like a bat? How did your arm feel when you made it like a jump rope?"

The creative person can produce a discussion that will increase an understanding of the relaxation phenomenon. This is but one example and one is limited only by his or her own imagination in developing others.

THE QUIETING REFLEX

The Quieting Reflex Concept (QR) was discovered several years ago by Dr. Charles F. Stroebel, Director of Research, Institute of Living, and Professor of Psychiatry, University of Connecticut Medical School, Hartford, Connecticut. This was an outgrowth of his work using bio-feedback to treat stress disorders in a clinic population ranging from age seven to seventy. His staff was amazed at the ease with which young members of the population acquired body skills that older patients found increasingly difficult with age. This was particularly true in the transfer into the real world with its inevitable stresses and worries.

Initially, the six-second QR was designed to help adults not "just relax," but to automatically adjust their body tension up and down to meet the actual stress at hand. After six months' practice, QR remarkably increased their ability to avoid and eliminate stress illnesses.

QR is designed to teach people an important life skill, namely, the Quieting Reflex. It can help them live more productive, less stressful lives, while at the same time, enhancing their healthiness and their potentials by reducing the negative effects of inappropriately perceived stress. Thus, the purpose of the QR program is to help individuals approach the unavoidable demands of life in a way in which they can feel better about themselves and others and to live appropriately less stress-ful lives.

Dr. Stroebel likens the fight or flight response, which was discussed previously, as being similar to the gear in a car. The passing gear is a wonderful emergency safety mechanism. When you get into a tight spot, you can push the accelerator to the floor and zoom out of the problem. At the same time, if you drive your car in passing gear all the time, it will wear out. Obviously, this is not a very effective way to use an automobile. The same is true for our bodies. We should not stay in passing gear unnecessarily.

The problem with many people is that they learn how to overuse the passing gear; and, eventually they do not know how to get out of passing gear. Simply telling a person "not to worry" or "Just take it easy" is not satisfactory because most people do not understand what it means to "just relax," nor do they know how to "not worry."

For the most part, stressful concerns require mental rather than the physical caveman type of response, yet people often use their fight or flight reaction in the absence of immediate physical threat. Inappropriate use of the fight or flight emergency response lessens the mental alertness people need to solve whatever problem is causing stress. This overuse of the fight or flight response is clearly inappropriate or maladaptive.

Many individuals inadvertently learn to activate the emergency response at the slightest sign and, therefore, repeatedly use this mechanism inappropriately. This panic reaction may then prevent them from performing appropriately, and from responding to their true potentials. In other words, the stress reaction acts as a block of learning and other life pursuits (actual laboratory body measurements of persons indicate that most of them have a quick panic reaction, lasting from six to ten seconds, and this reduces their ability to perform optimally).

Many people develop or maintain a high level of arousal much more frequently and for a much longer period than they should. Bodies of healthy people should quickly recover normal balance after their initial reaction to stress. This is the body's inherent quieting reaction, or Quieting Reflex. However, many individuals have unconsciously taught their bodies to override their own natural quieting responses until constant tension, anxiety, and tightness begin to seem normal to them.

What the QR program is all about is a contrary response to the passing gear or emergency reaction. This contrary response is called the Quieting Reflex. It begins in early training phases as a response to things that get on people's nerves, that annoy them, or that get them frustrated or angry. With progressive practice, individuals can acquire a virtually reflexive ability to produce a set of behaviors that are actually contrary to the inappropriate use of the passing gear. The two obviously cannot happen simultaneously, so there has now been produced a new adaptive state where individuals do not have to get their bodies upset when it is not appropriate.

The emergency reaction involves approximately five steps. The first is increased vigilance or paying attention to what is potentially harmful in the environment; that is, to whatever is feared. Frequently, almost simultaneously, with this, there is a blush reaction, a wetness of the hands, or a tendency towards perspiration. Almost simultaneously comes a perking of attention and a tension of the musculature of the face. The face becomes grim. At about three seconds into this passing gear emergency response, there is a catching or holding of the breath or there is shallow, quick breathing, almost panting. The next change frequently is a drop in hand temperature. The hands and often the feet become cold and clammy. And, finally, the jaw is clenched much like a dog going into battle. These changes can be easily measured by laboratory instrumentation.

The Quieting Reflex is a reversal of these steps. The first thing that happens in the Quieting Reflex is that the person becomes aware that something is annoying him, making him tense or anxious. He learns how to monitor his body to determine what cues trigger off this emergency response, and then he learns a systematic way to reverse the Emergency Reaction by eliciting the Quieting Reflex. Thus, instead of being dependent upon tranquilizers or other drugs, young people and adults can use the six-second technique as a way of keeping their bodies calm when they really do not have to stand their ground and fight or run away.

It has been found that QR training helps people regain the capacity they had as younger children to recover quickly from excessive stress. In the course of training, young people learn to recognize when they are over-reacting to stress and learn specific techniques to bring their bodies back to a healthy level of activity. Later in training, they learn to apply these skills consciously in day-to-day school or job situations. Eventually, through repeated practice, the quieting technique becomes the body's automatic and unconscious response to stressful situations. When an emergency response is inappropriate, the body automatically responds with a QR.

It has also been found that a great majority of individuals, as they become proficient in evoking the Quieting Reflex, gain a new sense of freedom. They recognize that many of the problems that have disturbed them in the past are not beyond their voluntary control. Their new sense of mastery with QR leads to enhanced self-concept and an ability to use their full potential in ways that were previously thought to be impossible.

All of the relaxation procedures in this chapter have been used with varying degrees of success when appropriately applied with older adults. However, it is important to repeat that what may be satisfactory for one person may not necessarily be so for another.

Chapter 8

REDUCING STRESS THROUGH MEDITATION

The Eastern art of meditation dates back more than 2,000 years. Until recently this ancient art has been encumbered with religious as well as cultural connotations. In the 1960s, countercultures began using it as a route to a more natural means of living and relaxing. Today, persons from all walks of life can be counted among the untold numbers around the world who practice and realize the positive effects that meditation can have upon the human mind and body. This chapter will take into account various aspects of meditation, including various types of meditation, information about a procedure that can be easily learned and practiced for the purpose of reducing stress, and some scientific evidence that supports the use of meditation as a stress reduction technique.

It has been asserted by Kenneth Pelletier[25] that meditation should be defined as an experimental exercise involving an individual's actual attention, not belief systems or other cognitive processes, and that it should not be confused with prolonged, self-induced lethargy. The nervous system needs intensity and variety of external stimulation to maintain proper functioning.

Robert Woolfolk and Frank Richardson,[76] another authoritative source, suggest that at the very least meditation can give the mind a rest—a brief vacation from stress and worry, one that requires neither a travel agent nor days free from the responsibility of work or family. It is almost as though meditation allows us to temporarily shut down those information-processing mechanisms of the brain that are ultimately responsible for producing stress. In addition, this short vacation from stress rests and revitalizes our coping abilities, giving us a more balanced outlook and increased energy for dealing with whatever difficulties face us.

Although there are many meditation techniques, *concentration* is an important factor contributing to success in most of them. The mind's natural flow from one idea to another is quieted by the individual's concentration. Lowering mental activity may be an easy task, but almost total elimination of scattered thoughts takes a great deal of time and practice on the part of the meditator.

The question sometimes raised is, "Are sleep and meditation the same thing?" Sleep has been likened to meditation, as both are hypometabolic states; that is, restful states where the body experiences decreased metabolism. But meditation is not a form of sleep. Although some similar psychological changes have been found in sleep and meditation, they are not the same and one is not a substitute for the other. In this regard, it is interesting to note that various studies have shown that meditation may restore more energy than sleep.

There have been countless positive pronouncements about meditation from some of the most notable scientists of modern times, who spend a good portion of their time studying about stress. However, it has been in relatively recent years only that the scientific community has uncovered many of the positive effects that the repeated practice of meditation has upon those who are stress ridden. Various scientific studies have shown that meditation can actually decrease the possibilities of an individual contracting stress-related disorders, and that meditators have a much faster recovery rate when exposed to a stressful situation than non-meditators. Specifically, from a physiological point of view, Herbert Benson[69] has found that meditation decreases the body's metabolic rate, with the following decreases in bodily function involved: (1) oxygen consumption, (2) breathing rate, (3) heart rate and blood pressure, (4) sympathetic nervous system activity, and (5) blood lactate (a chemical produced in the body during stressful encounters). Also, meditation tends to increase the psychological ability of those who practice it, as well as to reduce anxiety. Research seems to be disclosing that meditation can be a path to better health (later in the chapter we will examine some of this scientific inquiry in more detail).

TYPES OF MEDITATION

Having made a rather thorough examination of the literature on meditation, I have been able to identify more than 20 meditational systems. Interestingly enough, although there are many meditation techniques, one notable researcher, Daniel Goleman,[77] has concluded that research tends to show that one technique is about as good as another for improving the way we handle stress.

I have arbitrarily selected for discussion here, four types of meditation:

(1) Christian meditation, (2) Meditative-running, (3) Strategic meditation, and (4) Transcendental meditation.

Christian Meditation

If you ask the average person about meditation the response will ordinarily be that it is concerned with "sitting and thinking," or "engaging in silent prayer." And, basically this is essentially what Christian meditation means. According to Herbert Benson,[69] the roots of Christian meditation can be explained as follows:

> Christian meditation and mysticism were well developed within the Byzantine church and known as Hesychasm. Hesychasm involved a method or repetitive prayer which was described in the 14th century at Mount Athos in Greece by Gregory of Sinai and was called "The Prayer of the Heart" or "The Prayer of Jesus." It dates back to the beginnings of Christianity. The prayer itself was called secret meditation and was transmitted from older to younger monks through an initiation rite. Emphasis was placed on having a skilled instructor. The method of prayer recommended by these monks was to sit down alone and in silence. Lower your head, shut your eyes, breathe out gently, and imagine yourself looking into your own heart. Carry your mind, i.e., your thoughts, from your head to your heart. As you breathe out, say "Lord Jesus Christ, have mercy on me." Say it moving your lips gently, or simply say it in your mind. Try to put all other thoughts aside. Be calm, be patient, and repeat the process very frequently.

In modern times this ritual is not so pronounced and one feels he or she is meditating by reflecting upon certain experiences and evaluating certain activities that have taken place in his or her life. It may be recalled that I reported previously that about 10% of the older adults in my surveys indicated that they used meditation as a means of coping with stress. No doubt many of these individuals engaged in some form of Christian meditation as previously described.

Meditative Running

Two prominent researchers, Diane and Robert Hales,[78] have reported on a concept that has to do with a combination of meditation and running and what I would describe as meditative running. Although running and meditation seem like completely opposite states—one strenuous and the other serene—both can be considered as paths to altered states of consciousness, and together they can profoundly affect both body and mind. It is interesting that exercisers who meditate as they work out literally change the way their heart and lungs function. They burn less oxygen and use energy more efficiently. It is known that Tibetan monks, using a similar approach and concentrating on a mantra, have run distances of 300 miles over mountain trails in less than 30 hours.

The Hales also reported on the work of Dr. Earl Solomon, a psychiatrist at Harvard Medical School, and his research assistant, Ann Bumpus, who adapted Benson's meditation technique so that the runner can elicit the relaxation response with eyes open and feet moving. They suggest the following:

1. Run at a gentle, regular pace, effortlessly, almost mechanically.
2. Deeply relax all your muscles, starting with your feet and working up to your face.
3. Breathe in long—through your nose if you can—breathe out short and sharp through your mouth.
4. Repeat a mantra or phrase silently to yourself as you exhale.
5. Don't worry about your state of relaxation; let it come at its own pace.
6. Overcome distracting thoughts by focusing on a mantra.
7. Remain vigilant to any external danger, such as an approaching bus, car, or bicycle.

As a firm believer and active participant in both running and meditation, I can heartily endorse the combination of these two tried-and-true stress-reducing techniques. Of course, this is a personal opinion and one that works very well for me. However, I would be reluctant to impose my position on others.

Strategic Meditation

Amarjit S. Sethi,[79] one of my authors in my series on *Stress in Modern Society*, has developed the concept of Strategic meditation. He defines it as a process of balancing "calculative thinking" and "non-calculative thinking." In order to give specificity to this concept he has labeled it "Strategic meditation" so that it may be distinguished from other forms of meditation. The meditational process takes place in different contexts, comprising both the facts and the values of a given environment. The study of interactions between facts and values in shaping calculative and non-calculative thinking becomes a process of strategic meditation. It is strategic because meditation examines problems, identifies their nature, and establishes perspective. It is meditational because a person transforms the problem-solving orientation through a focus on both the problem and its solution, and this begins to suggest elements of how an individual processes information in a relatively "problem-free context" which has been termed non-calculative. Another term for such a level of consciousness is *playfulness*. The emphasis, in a meditational exercise, shifts from complex calculation and sophisticated decision rules to selective perception, leading to a problem-free context.

In order to practice strategic meditation one needs to develop his or her own diagnosis of the problem. Problem-solving is utilized as a process of investigating the source of stress, and is integrated as a part of the meditational process. This phase involves perception of the environment, analysis of the problem, and design of alternative solutions. The problem-solving process is integrated with a meditational process.

Transcendental Meditation

Of the various types of meditation, transcendental meditation (TM) is by far the best known. It was introduced in the United States many years ago by Mararishi Yogi. It is believed that he used the term transcendental (a literal meaning of which is "going beyond") to indicate that it projects one beyond the level of a wakeful experience to a state of profound rest along with heightened alertness.[80]

TM involves the repitition of a *mantra* (a word or specific sound) for 15 to 20 minutes daily with the meditator in a relaxed position with eyes closed. Almost without exception those who have practiced TM attest to its positive effects. While other forms of meditation may have specific procedures, it is safe to say that most derive in some way from basic TM. The discussion that follows is based on this type of meditation.

A PROCEDURE FOR MEDITATING

Presented here is a description of a procedure for meditating that I have found has met with personal success. In addition, many of my students have reported success with its use. Also, I have been able to apply it with success in working with many older adults. However, it should be mentioned that it is pretty much an individual matter, and what may be successful for one person may not necessarily be successful for another.

To begin with, there are certain basic considerations that should be taken into account. The following descriptive list of these considerations is general in nature, and the reader can make his or her own specific application as best fits individual needs and interests.

Locate a Quiet Place and Assume a Comfortable Position. The importance of a quiet environment should be obvious since concentration is facilitated in a tranquil surrounding. The question of the position one may assume for meditation is an individual matter. However, when it is suggested that one assume a comfortable position, this might be amended by, "but not too comfortable." The reason for this is that if one is too comfortable there is the possibility of falling asleep, and this of course would defeat the purpose of meditation. This is a reason why one should consider not taking a lying position while meditating.

A position might be taken where there is some latitude for "swaying." This can provide for a comfortable posture and, at the same time, guard against the individual "falling into dreamland." The main consideration is that the person be in a comfortable enough position to remain this way for a period of 15 minutes or so. One such position would be where you sit on the floor with legs crossed and the back straight and resting on the legs and buttocks. Your head should be erect and the hands resting in the lap. If you prefer to sit in a chair rather than on the floor, select a chair with a straight back. You need to be the judge of comfort, and, thus, you should select a position where you feel you are able to concentrate and remain in this position for a period of time.

Focus Your Concentration. As mentioned before, concentration is the essential key to successful meditation. If you focus on one specific thing, such as an object or a sound or a personal feeling, it is less likely that your thoughts will be distracted. You might want to consider focusing on such things as a fantasy trip, re-experiencing a trip already taken, a place that has not been visited, or a certain sound or chant.

Use a Nonsense Word or Phrase. Some techniques of meditation, such as the popular transcendental meditation, involve the chanting of a particular word (mantra) as one meditates. While the mantra has important meaning for the meditator, I refer to it as a nonsense word because it should be devoid of any connotation that would send one thinking in many directions. This, of course, would hinder concentration, so a nonsense word would perhaps be most effective. Incidentally, I have found in my own personal experience with meditation, the practice of chanting such a word is very effective.

Be Aware of Natural Breathing Rhythm. The importance of natural breathing rhythm should not be underestimated. In fact, some clinical psychologists recommend this as a means of concentrating. That is, one can count the number of times he or she inhales and exhales, and this in itself is a relaxing mental activity.

The Time for Meditation. Since meditation is an activity to quiet the mind it is strongly recommended that the practice not be undertaken immediately at the end of the day. At this time, the mind may be in a very active state of reviewing the day's activities. My own personal experience suggests a 15 to 20 minute period in the morning and another such period in the evening preferably before dinner, or possibly two hours after dinner.

With the above basic considerations in mind, you should be ready to experiment. To begin with, assume a comfortable position in a quiet place with as passive an attitude as possible. Try to dismiss all wandering thoughts from your mind and concentrate on a relaxed body while keeping the eyes closed. When feeling fairly relaxed, the repetition of the nonsense word or phrase can begin. This can be repeated orally or silently. Personally, I have had good success repeating it silently; that is, through the mind. Repeat your chosen word or phrase in this manner over and over, keeping the mind clear of any passing thoughts. At first, this may be very difficult, but with practice, it becomes easier.

After a period of about 15 or 20 minutes have passed, (or less if you wish), discontinue repetition of the word or phrase. Become aware of your relaxed body once again. Give yourself a few moments before moving as your body will need to readjust. For successful prolonged results one might consider continuing the practice two times daily for 15 to 20 minute sessions.

If you have difficulty trying to meditate on your own, it is possible to seek the services of an experienced meditator for assistance and supervision. The recent more widespread popularity of meditation has been accompanied by the establishment of meditation centers for instruction in some communities.

SCIENTIFIC EVIDENCE SUPPORTING
THE BENEFITS OF MEDITATION

Since many people are not aware of the value of meditation and since many others suspect it as a rather "spooky" procedure, it seems fitting to impress upon the reader that it is a very important area of scientific research.

The phenomenon of meditation is not an easy one to study objectively. One of the primary reasons for this is that it is extremely difficult to control all of the variables inherent in a given situation. For example, the difference in length of meditation sessions as well as the degree of meditating experience of the subjects sometimes militates against obtaining researchable experimental and control groups. These limitations should be kept in mind when reading the following research reports. It should also be remembered that a very large number of studies in this area have been undertaken over the years. Those cited here are merely representative examples of this vast number.

In studying meditation as an intervention in stress reactivity, Goleman and Schwartz[81] used skin conductive measures (a process similar to the polygraph—lie detector) to study certain aspects of meditation. There were 60 subjects, 30 of whom had over two years of experience with TM. The other 30 were non-meditators. The subjects were randomly selected for participation in one of three conditions: (1) meditation, (2) relaxation with open eyes, and (3) relaxation with closed eyes. In the meditation group, both meditators and non-meditators were assigned. The meditators with experience engaged in TM, and those without experience (controls) were instructed in a simple version of TM. After practicing this for a period of 20 minutes, subjects were instructed to open their eyes and view a five-minute film designed to be used as a stressor. During meditation and while viewing the film, the subjects were measured for skin conductance and pulse rate. These measurements were recorded twice each minute. Experienced meditators showed more increase in skin conductance during the time immediately before the highly emotionally-charged part of the film. However, there was a decrease in this measurement after the film was viewed. These results could be interpreted to mean generally that those experienced in the practice of meditation can relieve stress by using this particular medium.

In studying the physiological effects of meditation Wallace[82] used subjects who had practiced meditation for a period of from six months to three years. The subjects sat with eyes open for five minutes. This was followed by a 15 minute period with closed eyes, and then for a one-half hour period they used TM. At the end of this time, they sat with closed eyes for 10 minutes followed by open eyes for five minutes.

Several physiological measurements were recorded during TM and the control periods. For the experimental period (TM), there was reduction in oxygen consumption by 16 percent. In addition, there was over a 14 percent reduction in carbon-dioxide elimination. These results were interpreted to mean that there was slowed metabolic rate and a state of deep rest (Basal Metabolic Rate—BMR is indicative of the speed at which body fuel is changed to energy, as well as how fast this energy is used; the BMR can be measured in terms of calories per meter of body surface with a calorie representing a unit measure of heat energy in food).

The researcher also made a comparison of the oxygen consumption reduction during meditation with a night's sleep, and this amounted to a difference of about nine percent. This seemed to justify a generalization that 20 minutes of meditation produced nearly two times the metabolic decrease during sleep. This could also be interpreted to mean that a deep state of relaxation could be obtained in a relatively short period of time by use of meditation.

Since much credence has been placed on stress reduction, in the control and resistance to disease, it seems appropriate to look at the specific technique of meditation in this regard. In consideration of the fact that the health of one's gums is assumed to be an acceptable criterion for overall health, and further, that gum inflammation seems related to stress levels, this condition appears to be a satisfactory medium for studying the general area of disease resistance. Klemons[83] undertook a study of this nature by examining 46 practicing meditators for common inflammation of the gums before and after a special course involving extended meditation. Significant improvement was reported for the meditators when compared to a control group of non-meditators. A conclusion that could be drawn is that a TM program increases resistance to disease if, as mentioned previously, gum inflammation can be accepted as a valid criterion.

An interesting study regarding reaction time and meditation was conducted by Shaw and Kolb.[84] Reaction time is the amount of time it takes from the time a signal is given until the initial movement (stimulus-response). This should not be confused with speed of movement, which is concerned with how fast the initial movement is completed.

In this study, the subjects were nine meditators with a like number of non-meditators as controls. All subjects reacted to a signal that was a flash of light. At this stimulus the subjects responded by pressing a button. The results showed that meditators tended to react faster than non-meditators by almost a 30 percent difference. Following such stimulus-response trials, all subjects took a 15 minute break period. During this time the meditators practiced TM and the non-meditators sat with eyes closed. On a retest of both groups, the meditators' reaction time was reduced 15 percent while the non-meditators' reaction time increased by about 10 percent.

Various generalizations could be drawn from this study. For example, one could be tempted to conclude that practicing meditation could improve coordination of mind and body.

In the next study Kirsch and Henry[85] asked 38 speech-anxious subjects to give a speech and their heart rates were assessed immediately before the speeches were given. They were assigned the following treatment strategies: (1) systematic desensitization, (2) desensitization and meditation replacing progressive relaxation, (3) meditation only, and (4) no treatment. All three treatment manuals included coping skill instructions. The results indicated that the three treatments were equally effective in reducing anxiety and produced a greater reduction in self-reported (but not behavioral) anxiety than that found in untreated subjects.

It was found that expectancy for improvement may have been a more important factor than coping devices themselves in reducing stress. The lack of significant differences between treatment groups suggests the viability of considering self-administered training in meditation, coupled with coping skill instructions, as an alternative to self-administered desensitization programs.

Hall and Goldstein[86] evaluated the effects of a behavioral approach (consisting of a relaxation exercise and meditational imagery) to disease by measuring selected physiological aspects of immune responsiveness in cancer patients. The exercise involved patients imagining that feeble cancer cells were crushed by stalwarts of the immune system. It was found that behavioral therapy amplified the immune system's response to disease; in physiological terms, it accelerated the rate of which lymphocytes mobilized to attack foreign bodies and possibly increased their own numbers. Although this study needs to be confirmed by further research, it does point to a correlation between meditation (mental states) and immunity.

In a study to determine the influence of meditation on the increased orderliness of thinking, Miskiman[87] used two groups of subjects: one of meditators and a control group that relaxed twice daily with closed eyes. After the first 40 days of the TM program, the meditators increased appreciably in their tendency to spontaneously organize memorized material in their minds. This was measured by the Index of Cluster in Recall. Members of the control group did not change significantly. Also, the organization of memory in meditators was stronger and more stable over a period of two to six months than was the case in the control group. The memories of the meditators decreased only three percent in recall efficiency while the memories of the non-meditators decreased 38 percent.

In the final study reported here, Tojoa[88] tried to determine the effect of meditation on intelligence. One year after 14 of the subjects began a TM program, he used the seven most regular meditators among them for the experimental group, with the control group consisting of non-meditators. He administered a neuroticism test and an intelligence test, with the result showing significant decrease in neuroticism and increase in intelligence in the experimental group and no significant changes in the non-meditating control group (it should be remembered that the difference was in an improved intelligence test score, which in itself is not necessarily a guarantee of improved intelligence).

The studies reported here comprise but a bare minimum of the large number that have been undertaken in the area of effectiveness of meditation. In all cases, these examples have shown very positive effects of meditation. However, it is repeated that certain precautions need to be taken into account in interpreting the results, and the reader is reminded again of the limitations that were mentioned at the outset of this discussion.

In closing this chapter, it is reiterated that whether or not one chooses meditation as a technique for stress reduction is an individual matter. It might be recalled that I reported previously that a relatively small number of the older adults (10%) in my surveys used meditation as a means of coping with stress; however, all of these respondents reported great success with the technique and recommended it for others.

Chapter 9

INDUCING THE RELAXATION
RESPONSE THROUGH BIOFEEDBACK

In this discussion of biofeedback I want to make it luminously clear that we are dealing with a complex and complicated subject. It will be the purpose to discuss this phenomenon in terms of what it is supposed to be and what it is supposed to do. It should be borne in mind that in biofeedback training (BFT), an important factor is that it take place under qualified supervision. This means that should you wish to pursue an interest in, and eventually participate in BFT, you should seek the services of one trained in this area.

In my surveys of older adults less than one percent reported experience with biofeedback. However, in my lectures on stress to senior citizen groups the subject of biofeedback frequently comes up and they are eager to have information about it. Some have had friends who have had experience with the practice and, interestingly enough, some of these persons are *diabetes mellitus* patients.

Lilian Rosenbaum,[89] a contributor to Volume 1 of my *Human Stress: Current Selected Research* has done an appreciable amount of experimentation with diabetes and stress. She has found that with people suffering from diabetes, stress does play a part in their lives and in their diabetes control.

In one of her studies reported in my series on *Stress and Modern Society*,[90] six insulin-treated diabetes patients completed a biofeedback program based on family systems theory. They improved their response to life stressors and none had negative effects. Four decreased their insulin requirement, one remained stable during two pregnancies, and the sixth became stable and discontinued drug abuse.

THE MEANING OF BIOFEEDBACK

The term *feedback* has been used in various frames of reference. It may have been used originally in engineering in connection with control systems that involve feedback procedures. These feedback control systems make adjustments to environmental changes, such as the case of your thermostat controlling temperature levels in your home.

Learning theorists use the term feedback interchangeably with the expression *knowledge of results* to describe the process of providing the learner with information as to how accurate his reactions were. Or, in other words, feedback is knowledge of various kinds that the performer received about his performance. With particular reference to motor skill learning, some psychologists reported many years ago that feedback in the form of knowledge of results is the strongest, most important variable controlling performance and learning, and, further, that studies have repeatedly shown that there is no improvement without it, progressive improvement with it, and deterioration after its withdrawal.[91]

According to Barbara Brown,[92] one of the foremost authorities on the subject of biofeedback, the terms *feedback* and *feedback control systems* were borrowed by physiologists when they began theorizing about how the functions of the body were performed. Modern writers on the subject of biofeedback seem to describe it in essentially the same way although some may elaborate more in determining its precise meaning. That is, some merely state what it is, while others may extend the description to include what it does. For example, one source[93] describes it as any information that we receive about the functioning of our internal organs such as the heart, sweat glands, muscles, and brain. Another similar description[94] indicates that it is a process in which information about an organism's biologic activity is supplied for perception by the same organism. Another source[95] extends this some by indicating that biofeedback is the monitoring of signals from the body, such as muscle tension and hand warmth, and the feeding of this information back through the use of sophisticated machines to individuals so they can get external information as to exactly what is happening in their bodies.

There are perhaps millions of individual feedback systems in the human body, and information about the external environment is sensed by way of the five senses and relayed to a control center, usually the brain, where it is integrated with other relevant information. When the sensed information is significant enough, central control generates commands for appropriate body changes.

These senses can also be thought of as the systems of *perception;* that is, how we obtain information from the environment and what we make of it. Learning theorists agree that the forms of perception most involved in learning are *auditory* perception, *visual* perception, *kinesthetic* perception, and *tactile* perception. Auditory perception is the mental interpretation of what a person hears. Visual perception is the mental interpretation of what a person sees. Kinesthetic perception is the mental interpretation of the sensation of body movement. Tactile perception is the mental interpretation of what a person experiences through the sense of touch. In this regard, it is common practice among learning theorists to refer to auditory feedback, visual feedback, kinesthetic feedback, and tactile feedback.

BIOFEEDBACK INSTRUMENTATION

We are all aware of the fact that the human body itself is a complicated and complex biofeedback instrument, which alerts us to certain internal activity, as mentioned in the previous discussion. However, many students of the subject feel that there is still a need for sensitive instruments to monitor physiological and psychological reactivity. Following is a brief discussion of the more widely known biofeedback instruments that are used both for research and therapeutic purposes.

Electromyograph (EMG)

Electromyography is the recording of electric phenomena occurring in muscles during contraction. Needle or skin electrodes are used and connected with an oscilloscope so that action potentials may be viewed and recorded (the oscilloscope is an instrument that visually displays an electrical wave on a fluorescent screen). Before the electromyograph was available, guesswork ordinarily had to be used to try to determine the participation of the muscles in movement. When a muscle is completely relaxed or inactive, it has no electric potential; however, when it is engaged in contraction, current appears.

It is believed that EMG training can produce deep muscle relaxation and relieve tension. A person gets the feedback by seeing a dial or hearing a sound from the machine, and he knows immediately the extent to which certain muscles may be relaxed or tensed. A muscle frequently used in EMG training for research and other purposes is the *frontalis* located in the front of the head.

Another important aspect of EMG is that which is concerned with retraining a person following an injury or disease when there is a need to observe small increments of gain in function of a muscle.

Feedback Thermometers

The obvious purpose of feedback thermometers is to record body temperatures. Ordinarily, a thermistor is attached to the hands or fingers. This highly sensitive instrument shows very small increments of degrees of temperature change so that the person receives the information with a visual or auditory signal. This kind of feedback instrumentation has been recommended for such purposes as reduction of stress and anxiety and autonomic nervous system relaxation.

Electroencephalograph (EEG)

The purpose of this instrument is to record amplitude and frequency of brain waves, and it has been used in research for many years. It has also been used with success to diagnose certain clinical diseases. In addition, EEG feedback has found use in psychotherapy, and in reducing stress as well as pain.

An interesting relatively recent horizon for EEG feedback is how it might be involved in creativity and learning. In fact, some individuals involved in creative activity have indicated that they can emerge from the EEG *theta* state with answers to problems that they previously were unable to solve. The theta waves are ordinarily recorded when a person is in a state of drowsiness or actually falling asleep. It is perhaps for this reason that this condition has been referred to by some as "sleep learning." Since it is a state just before sleep, others refer to it as the twilight period or *twilight learning.*

Galvanic Skin Response (GSR)

There are several different kinds of GSR instruments used to measure changes in electrical resistance of the skin to detect emotional arousal. The instrument reacts in proportion to the amount of perspiration one emits and the person is informed of the changes in electrical resistance by an auditory or visual signal. One aspect of GSR is concerned with the use of the polygraph or lie detector, which is supposed to record a response that is concerned with lying. GSR feedback is oftentimes recommended for use of relaxation, reducing tension, improvement of ability to sleep, or for emotional control.

In general, the purpose of the biofeedback machinery is to provide accurate and reliable data that will increase one's awareness of how the body is functioning and demonstrate one's influence of his action of his body. Hopefully, this information should be useful in inspiring a person to take an active self-interest in his own well-being. After such information is received, if it has been obtained under the supervision of a qualified person, there may be a given number of sessions arranged for consultation and training. Perhaps the ultimate objective is for the individual to be able to gain control over his own autonomic nervous system.

As popular and well-advertised as biofeedback machinery has become, it is not without its critics. One such authority on mind-body relationships is Beata Jencks,[54] who feels that many important purposes can be accomplished without instruments by using the body as its own biofeedback instrument. In fact, she identifies over a dozen of these, including the following: (1) diverse muscle relaxation, (2) change of heart rate and body temperature, (3) change of breathing patterns, (4) decrease of stress and anxiety reactions, (5) mental relaxation, (6) autonomic nervous system relaxation, (7) pain relief for tension headaches, backaches, and other aches and pains, and (8) improved learning ability, including enhancement of concentration and recall. She indicates, however, that certain of the biofeedback instruments, particularly EMG has important application for retraining of patients following disease and injury.

At the present time, it is difficult to determine unequivocally what the future of biofeedback may be. Without question, it has influenced our way of thinking with reference to a person being able to possibly control his physiological functions. In view of this, perhaps one of its foremost contributions is that it creates in an individual a feeling of his own responsibility for his personal well-being.

In concluding this chapter, it is worth repeating that the practice of biofeedback should take place under the supervision of a qualified person. Also, if a disease syndrome is present a physician's referral may be required.

Chapter 10

CONTROLLING STRESS
THROUGH BEHAVIOR MODIFICATION

Included among numerous antonymous proverbs are: "You can't teach an old dog new tricks" and "You're never too old to learn." I happen to be a firm believer in the latter. My experience with older adults, as well as my own personal experience, assures me that more often than not older persons accused of being "set in their ways," are no more so than those of a younger age. Thus, behavior change can occur as well in older adults as it can at any age level.

For purposes of this discussion *behavior* will be considered as anything that the organism does as a result of some sort of stimulation. The term *modification* means a change in the organism caused by environmental factors. Thus, when the two terms are used together—behavior modification—they are interpreted to mean some sort of change in the way a person has ordinarily reacted to a given stimulus.

It is not uncommon for some individuals to display behavior that directly or indirectly causes stress arousal, either for themselves and/or for the person(s) toward whom the behavioral action is directed. It is the function of this chapter to provide information that will assist older adults to modify behavior for the purpose of correcting or at least improving upon this condition.

In recent years, behavior modification has become so broad in scope that it is used in many frames of reference. I would like to emphasize at this point that, for my purposes, I am not considering it as a variety of psychological and/or psychiatric techniques (therapist-client relations) for altering behavior. On the contrary, my recommendations for the use of modification of behavior are confined to its possibilities as a means to reduce certain stress-connected factors involved in a person's environment. This is to say that if one manifests a behavior that provokes a stressful situation, if he or she can change this behavior, it could be possible to eliminate, or at least minimize, the stressful condition.

In general, the practice of behavior modification involves external assistance as in the case of a nurse trying to effect a change in a patient, or a teacher trying to effect a change in a student. The major concern here is in the direction of *self*-modification, with a person attempting to improve his or her own behavior. This assumes that, generally speaking, individuals can help themselves develop the ability to increase desirable or appropriate behavior and to decrease undesirable or inappropriate behavior. Of course, this involves *self-control*, which can be described as manipulation of environmental events that influence one's own behavior for the purpose of changing the behavior. Self-control can eventually lead to behavioral self-management, which can be considered as the learning and practice of new habits. Satisfactory self-control and successful self-management are obviously contingent upon some sort of understanding of self, and this is the subject of the ensuing discussion.

TOWARD AN UNDERSTANDING OF SELF

In order to put an understanding of self in its proper perspective, consideration needs to be given to the basic aspects of *self-structure* and *self-concept*. The late Hugh Perkins,[96] one of my former associates and a leading learning theorist suggested that self-structure is the framework of a particular individual's complex of motives, perceptions, cognitions, feelings, and values—the product of developmental processes. Self-structure is revealed in behavior. One reveals in behavior the knowledge, skills, and interests that have been acquired, the goals being sought, the beliefs, values, and attitudes adopted, the roles learned, and the self-concept that has been formed. Thus, self-concept is an aspect of self-structure.

Among the most relevant and significant perceptions that an individual acquires are those of himself or herself in various life situations; and, further, that basically, the self-concept is made up of a large number of *percepts*, each of which contains one or more qualities that one ascribes to himself or herself. To be more specific, *self-percept* pertains to sense impressions of a trait ascribed to, while *self-concept* consists of the totality of one's self-percepts organized in some sort of order.

The frame of reference of self-concept with which I am concerned is the *total personality* concept. A great deal of clinical and experimental evidence indicates that a human being must be considered as a whole and not a collection of parts, and thus, is a total personality.

A question to raise is, "What comprises the total personality?" Anyone who has difficulty formulating views with regard to what the human personality actually consists of can take courage in the knowledge that many experts who spend their time studying it are not always in complete agreement as to what it is or how it operates. However, if one were to analyze the literature on the subject, it would be found generally, that the total personality consists of the sum of all the *physical, social, emotional* and *intellectual* aspects of any individual. This can also be expressed in terms of the physical self, social self, emotional self, and intellectual self with everyone manifesting certain kinds of physical behavior, social behavior, emotional behavior, and intellectual behavior. (Although this discussion deals with self-concept in a general way, as you read on, you will no doubt want to visualize the way in which "your own self" corresponds to the general pattern. The importance of this approach is seen when you as an individual make an effort in the direction of self modification of behavior.)

The total personality is one thing comprising the above major aspects. All of these components are highly interrelated and interdependent. All are important to the balance and health of the personality because only in terms of their health can the personality as a whole maintain a completely healthy state. The condition of any one aspect affects each other aspect to a degree, and, hence, the personality as a whole.

When a nervous person stutters or becomes nauseated, a mental state is not necessarily causing a physical symptom. On the contrary, a pressure imposed upon the organism causes a series of reactions, which include thought, verbalization, digestive processes, and muscular function. Mind does not always cause the body to become upset; the total organism is upset by a situation, and reflects its upset in several ways, including disturbance in thought, feeling, and bodily processes. The whole individual responds in interaction with the social and physical environment, and as the individual is affected by the environment, he or she in turn has an effect upon it.

It is interesting in modern times, when great emphasis is placed upon social adjustment, that perhaps a major problem involves faulty interpersonal relationships. For this reason, it is important to make special note of the interaction between the individual and the environment. The quality of the individual's interpersonal relationships affects all other aspects of his or her personality. How well do you drive a car when someone is shouting at you? How well can you concentrate when you think someone is talking about you? These are social circumstances that affect the physical, social, emotional, and intellectual aspects of personality.

All of these things, then, are the basis of total personality—a complex balance of psychological and social considerations that prepares the individual for the fullest, most socially valuable, productive and adventuresome living. A large portion of the responsibility falls to the individual to make those kinds of modifications in personal behavior that will in one way or another add to the quality of living and help in the prevention of undesirable stress.

SOME GENERAL PROCEDURES FOR SELF-MODIFICATION OF BEHAVIOR

Over the last several years a voluminous amount of literature has been published in the general area of behavior modification. Some of this has been directed to school administrators, teachers, counselors and others for the purpose of utilizing the procedure to produce behavior change in *others*. As mentioned before, I am concerned here with *self*-modification of behavior, and literature in this specific area is becoming more abundant.

Although self-modification of behavior is considered to be a relatively recent innovation, one report suggests that it was used in the early history of our country by Benjamin Franklin.[97] He is said to have used it to improve upon such virtues as temperance and frugality. He kept a record of errors he thought he made each day in each of over a dozen virtues. At the end of the day, he would consult the information to get feedback to help him identify those virtues he may have been violating. Of course, in modern times our approach to self-modification of behavior is much more sophisticated than that of Franklin, and improvement is constantly being made.

Whether one is attempting to modify behavior of another or trying to modify his or her own behavior, the general procedure of application is essentially the same. There are certain sequential steps to be taken that involve the following: (1) identification and description of one's behaviors, (2) counting behaviors, (3) attempting to effect a change in behaviors, and (4) evaluating the procedures used to change behaviors. The following discussion will take into account some of the important features involved in these various steps.

Identifying Behaviors

The first step in the process is concerned with identification of a behavior that one wishes to modify. This process is also referred to as *pin-pointing, targeting* or *specifying* a behavior. Essentially this involves trying to define a particular behavior (target) that one wishes to change. This is not always an easy matter because sometimes a person may manifest a behavior that is annoying to others, but he or she may be completely unaware of it.

When a person is able to identify a particular behavior and admit that such a behavior may be interfering with social relationships, a strong beginning can be made in the direction of behavioral change. In other words, recognizing that one has a problem is the first prerequisite to solving it.

In many instances, the identification of a behavior emerges when one is dissatisfied with what one may be doing. For example a person may be performing a behavior he or she does not want to perform, or not be performing a behavior he or she wants to perform.

Counting Behaviors

The second step in self-modification of behavior is concerned with actually counting how often a target behavior occurs. This means that one obtains a frequency count of the behavior to be improved. If this step is not taken, it is difficult to learn the extent to which the behavior is being performed. Sometimes, simply counting a behavior will tend to improve it because the person is becoming involved in self-awareness of the behavior. This is to say that counting a behavior calls one's attention to it and how often it is occuring.

In addition to determining the frequency of a behavior, another aspect of this step is what is sometimes called the *ABC Factor* in the behavior modification approach. That is, *A*ntecedent of the behavior, the *B*ehavior itself, and the *C*onsequence of the behavior. *Antecedent* is concerned with any event that preceded the behavior and *consequence* is what happens as a result of the behavior.

Obviously, it is most important that a person develop an awareness of antecedents and consequences of behaviors. The main reason for this is that an antecedent gets a behavior started and a given behavior can result as an unsatisfactory consequence.

Attempting to analyze an antecedent becomes important in terms of a manifested behavior. That is, why did the antecedent occur in the first place?

The information derived from step two in self-modification of behavior is usually designated as *baseline data.* If the information is valid and the behavior frequency is accurate, the person has a base from which to operate. This means that one should be in a position to see if attempts at improving a given behavior—step three, *changing behavior* is meeting with satisfactory results.

Changing Behaviors

Any effort to change a behavior that has been identified, described, counted, and recorded is referred to as a *plan of intervention.* That is, the person intervenes with one or more procedures designed to modify the inappropriate behavior. Any plan to replace an inappropriate behavior with an appropriate one involves some sort of reinforcement procedure. Generally speaking, *self*-reinforcement is concerned with changing behavior through *self*-produced consequences, and these consequences may be overt or covert. Examples are statements to oneself or the acquisition of an item as a reward for one's efforts.

Evaluating the Plan of Intervention

The final step in self-modification of behavior is concerned with how well the plan of intervention is succeeding; that is, the extent to which the changes in behavior are achieving desired results. This process requires the development of valid evaluative criteria. These criteria can be broad in scope, and thus apply to any problem of self-modification of behavior, or they can be more specific and be applied to a particular case. Some examples of general criteria might include the following:

1. In general, was there an increase in appropriate behavior and/or a decrease in inappropriate behavior?
2. What were the behaviors that achieved the most satisfactory results?
3. What forms of reinforcement appeared to be most successful?

Whatever way one decides to evaluate the plan of intervention, there is still another decision to be made. This also concerns the extent to which the plan has achieved success. If it has met with complete and unequivocal success, it can then perhaps be terminated. Or, if it succeeds only when the behavior change is still being practiced, there may be need to maintain the procedure. Perhaps the ultimate goal should be to modify behavior to the extent that the problem would be completely eliminated. This can be accomplished if one conscientiously and systematically carries out the general procedures outlined above. Experiences have shown that older adults can modify their own behavior not only to correct stress arousal but to avoid it as well. The following is a case in point.

A CASE OF BEHAVIOR
MODIFICATION OF AN OLDER ADULT

Over the years, 72-year-old George had gained a reputation among his friends and neighbors as one who liked to monopolize the conversation. In fact, to some he was a downright braggadocio—sometimes to the extent that his presence became obnoxious to others. His family of adult children and particularly his wife would tolerate this behavior not fully realizing that it was not placing George very high on the social acceptance scale. Often to the consternation of others in a group, his wife would defer to him as he picked up on an anecdote that she had begun to relate. This, of course, did not add to George's already low ebb of popularity.

Several months ago George had experienced one of life's most stressful events—the death of his wife of 43 years. With the loss of his wife George became more and more dejected until his son and daughter convinced him that it might be in his best interest to move into a retirement resort in a nearby community.

All seemed to go well with George in his new surroundings until he began to fall back into his old "conversation-monopolyzing self." Needless to say, this behavior became an unacceptable bore to many of the groups with which George had become associated. And, the last thing he needed at this stage of his life was rejection.

Margaret, a lady in one of the groups, although she did not approve of George's behavior, nevertheless felt that he did exude a certain amount of charm in his conversations. Margaret had had experience with this type before and was sure that George could be "rehabilitated." She sought out the cooperation of the social director of the retirement resort and they set about to help George change his behavior. Margaret and the social director met with George and told him point blank about the problem. To their surprise, George admitted to the shortcoming and agreed that he would like to improve on it; that is, modify his behavior. The behavior had been identified and the various steps in behavior modification were applied.

A plan was worked out whereby when George appeared to be "talking too much," Margaret would use a facial code signal to imply this to George. He would then find some reason to withdraw from the conversation by excusing himself to make a phone call or some other such excuse.

Before too long with the determination of George and the help of Margaret, his behavior changed at least enough for him to become an accepted member of the group.

SYSTEMATIC SELF-DESENSITIZATION

A form of behavior modification known as systematic desensitization can be described as the process of systematically lessening a specific learned fear in an individual. It is purported to provide one means of controlling anxiety. If one can accomplish this, it becomes an extremely important factor in reducing stress. The reason for this is that the individual becomes more able to control his or her fears and anxieties, rather than being controlled by them. From the point of view of a clinical psychotherapeutic procedure, systematic desensitization consists of presenting to the imagination of the deeply relaxed person the feeblest item in a list of anxiety-evoking stimuli repeatedly, until no more anxiety is evoked. The next item on the list is presented, and so on, until, eventually, even the strongest of the anxiety evoking stimuli fails to evoke any stir of anxiety in the person. It is the purpose here to provide information to help the reader understand the process of this technique and, at the same time, give consideration to self-administration for the ultimate purpose of reducing stress.

Originally, the focus of systematic desensitization was primarily upon counselor-client, therapist-patient, or teacher-student relationships, and it was perhaps one of the most widely used behavior therapy techniques. In recent years, systematic desensitization has gained great favor as a *self*-administered technique. Although the value of it as a means of lessening stress-provoking situations has not been completely established by behavioral scientists, some of the research findings are indeed encouraging. For example, studies have shown that systematic desensitization can be very effective in overcoming severe public speaking anxiety, test anxiety, and a host of other stress-invoking stimuli.

It is believed by many clinical psychologists that systematic self-desensitization efforts are not likely to be harmful, even if they fail. However, self-desensitization should be approached as an experimental procedure and it should be discontinued if the course of anxiety reduction is not relatively smooth, and it should be discontinued immediately if any increase in anxiety is experienced.

Systematic desensitization is based on the notion that many anxieties that people experience are due to what are termed *conditioned reactions.* These conditioned reactions can be identified as stimuli that occur together in our experience and become associated with each other so that we respond to them in the same way, or in a highly similar way, when they occur again. This is to say that if we are made anxious in the presence of certain stimuli these same stimuli will make us anxious later when they occur, even if the situation in reality no longer poses an actual threat. An example is a person who may have had a number of experiences as a child in which a person in authority, such as a school principal, policeman, or guard frightened him or her and was perhaps punished in some way. Such a person's reactions as an adult to one in authority may produce considerably more anxiety than the situation really justifies. This is because of previous conditioning of strong anxiety to an authority figure.

Many of our emotions seem to be based on such conditioned reactions. And, these reactions are somewhat similar to reflexes, but they are learned rather than inherited (the reader is asked to refer back to the discussion of learned and unlearned tensions in Chapter 2). Their automatic or "reflexive" character, however, explains why it is difficult to discuss things rationally with someone who is emotionally involved in a situation. Such a person is responding more with conditioned reactions to the present stimuli than relating to the actual realities of the situation.

The recommendation for overcoming anxieties in the form of conditioned reactions is the use of systematic self-desensitization and a highly persuasive case can be made for its effectiveness—provided it is done properly.

After a particular problem has been identified, the process consists of three sequential steps: (1) developing a hierarchy of anxiety-evoking stimuli, (2) complete relaxation, and (3) desensitization sessions. Using the previously mentioned authority figure example, I will explain how I made application of this to a nurse who was having difficulty with this problem where relationship with a given physician was concerned.[98]

The first step was to take several index cards, writing a different situation or experience on each card that made for anxiety concerning the problem. The cards were then stacked in order with the one causing the least anxiety on the top and the one causing the greatest anxiety at the bottom. This is the hierarchy of anxiety-evoking stimuli in this case and is listed as follows:

1. Entering the hospital parking lot and seeing the physician's car.
2. Greeting other nurses and discussing the physician.
3. Greeting a nurse who mentions her association with the physician.
4. Conferring with another nurse about her relationship with the physician.
5. Walking by physician's office when the door is closed.
6. Walking by physician's office when the door is open (no verbalization or eye contact).
7. Walking by physician's office when door is open using eye contact and nodding.
8. Arranging meeting with physician's secretary.
9. Talking with physician's secretary about the physician.
10. Prearranged meeting with physician with secretary present.
11. Prearranged meeting with physician with only self present.
12. Other meetings with the physician with only self present.

The second step was to try to develop a condition of complete relaxation (the reader should refer back to Chapter 7 about relaxation procedures).

After the nurse was completely relaxed, the next step was the beginning of systematic desensitization. This is done as follows: Look at the top card of the pile—the one that is the least anxiety provoking. Close the eyes, and, using the imagination, visualize as vividly as possible the situation described on it. That is, imagine the situation occurring and actually being there. At this point, if some anxiety is experienced, the imaginary scene should cease immediately and going back to relaxing. After complete relaxation is again obtained, continue the procedure. This is continued until the scene can be imagined without anxiety. This may take only one or two times, or it could take 15 to 20 times, but it should be repeated until no anxiety is felt. The entire procedure is continued until all the cards have been gone through.

It is recommended that work on the cards in this manner should be for approximately one-half hour at a time. It can be done daily, every other day, or a couple of times a week, depending upon the amount of time a person is willing or able to spend, and how quickly the person wants to conquer the anxiety. It appears to be a good practice to overlap one or two items from one session to another; that is, beginning a session by repeating an item or two from the previous session that were imagined without anxiety.

One variation of the above procedure is to tape record a description of each scene in advance. Then relax and listen to the tape. If anxiety appears, the recorder is turned off and going back to relaxing. When relaxation is again accomplished, proceed as before. A value of using the tape recorder is that there is likely to be better pronunciation, enunciation, and intonation of words. In addition, it may be easier to concentrate since it is one's own auditory input on tape and the person does not have the additional task of verbalizing and trying to concentrate on the scene at the same time. If desired, the sequence of relaxation procedures can be taped as well.

After a person has been desensitized, he or she can review in his or her own mind the preferred action to take in the situation that caused the anxiety. Plans can then be made to do the right thing the next time the situation occurs.

Obviously, the success experienced with this procedure will depend largely upon the extent to which a person is willing to make the painstaking effort involved in the approach. I have proposed this procedure to many older adults and those who have tried it have been so delighted by its effects that they have deliberately sought out situations that previously had caused them great anxiety, frustration and failure. This is certainly a true test of faith in the approach.

A CASE OF SELF-DESENSITIZATION OF AN OLDER ADULT

It was mentioned previously that systematic desensitization can be very effective in overcoming severe public speaking anxiety. In fact, the condition of "stage fright" is one that exists among many people—with some being much more susceptible to it than others. There is no question about it, "getting up in front of the class" can be a nemesis for some throughout life.

Alice, age 68, had been a shy person all of her life. She had wanted to be a high school mathematics teacher and prepared to do so during her college years. However, when it came to student teaching she found that she could not consistently stand before a group. Consequently, she used her mathematics training, and, with a few more courses, graduated with a degree in accounting. Upon completing her degree she acquired a position as an accountant and stayed with the same company until she retired at age 65. In this position, she rarely, if ever, had to face the encumbrance of "stage fright."

At the age of 68 Alice decided to become a member of a retirement residence that had been highly recommended to her. This residence had numerous social activities and members were free to select those of their choice. Alice decided to join the book club unaware that she would eventually be expected to give book reports to the group.

Soon she became somewhat stressed by the expectation that reporting before the group inevitably would have to be faced. Fortunately, she had befriended 71-year-old Cynthia, one of the residents who had been a clinical psychologist for over 30 years. When Alice told Cynthia about her problem the latter recommended the process of self-desensitization and together they worked out the following hierarchy of anxiety-evoking stimuli:

1. Reading an article about giving reports.
2. Reading report alone.
3. Reading report in front of a mirror.
4. Reading report into tape recorder and playing back.
5. Reading report to a friend, (Cynthia).
6. Reading report to Cynthia with one other present.
7. Reading report with three others present.
8. Reading report to two or three where there is a large gathering, such as the dining room.
9. Entering the room where the report is to be given.
10. Member of audience where reports are given.
11. Giving report to entire group.

The appropriate procedures for self-desensitization were applied and finally Alice had conquered her stage fright anxiety when she was nearing "three score and ten."

It has been the purpose of this book to provide the reader with an understanding about the complex and complicated problem of stress and how to cope with it. All of the techniques and recommendations throughout the book have met with varying degrees of success with older adults who have practiced them.

Individual differences indicate that one person may find more success than another with a given procedure. One of the most important factors to take into account is that dealing with stress is pretty much an individual matter. With practice, most of you will have some degree of success in your attempts to cope with your own stressful conditions. Above all, a positive attitude toward life in general is an essential prerequisite for any kind of stress management program that is undertaken.

REFERENCES

1. Julian, Teresa W., McKenny, Patrick C. and Kevin, Arnold, Psychological predictors of stress associated with the male midlife crisis, *Sex Roles*, June 1990, 707–722.
2. Luboudrov, S., Congressional perceptions of the elderly: The use of stereotypes in the legislative process, *The Gerentologist*, 27, 77–81, 1986.
3. U. S. Bureau of the Census, Current Population Reports, Series P-23, No. 138: *Demographic and Socioeconomic Aspects of Aging in the United States*, U. S. Government Printing Office, Washington, DC, 1984.
4. Morse, Donald R. and Pollack, Robert L., *Nutrition, Stress and Aging*, New York, AMS Press, Inc., No. 17 in series on Stress in Modern Society, James H. Humphrey, Editor, 1988, 144–157.
5. Feinson, Marjorie C. and Thoits, Peggy A. The distribution of stress among elders, *Journal of Gerontology*, March 1986, 225–233.
6. Jamison, Robert N., Sobrocco, Tracey and Parris, Winston C., The influence of problems with concentration and memory on emotional stress and daily activities in chronic pain patients. *International Journal of Psychiatry in Medicine*, 1988, Vol 18(2), 183–191.
7. Sands, James D., The relationship of stressful life events to intellectual functioning in women over 65. *International Journal of Aging and Human Development*, 1981–82, Vol. 14(1), 11–22.
8. Rosch, Paul J., Join us in the quest to better understand and manage the stress syndrome, *Practical Stress Management, the Newsletter of the American Institute of Stress*, September 1983.
9. *Human Stress: Current Selected Research*, Vol. 1, New York, AMS Press, James H. Humphrey, Editor, ix., 1986.
10. Steinhaus, Arthur, *Toward an Understanding of Health and Physical Education*, Dubuque, Iowa, William C. Brown, 1963, 75.
11. Walker, C. Eugene, *Learn to Relax: 13 Ways to Reduce Tension*, Englewood Cliffs, NJ, Prentice-Hall, 1975, 3.
12. Viscott, David, *The Language of Feelings*, New York, Arbor House, 1976, 51.
13. Caccese, Thomas M. and Mayerberg, Cathleen K., Gender differences in perceived burnout of college coaches, *Journal of Sport Psychology*, 6(3), Champaign, IL 1984.
14. Malone, Christopher J., and Rotella, Robert J., Preventing coaching burnout, *Journal of Health, Physical Education, Recreation and Dance*, November/December, 1981.

15. The New Columbia Encyclopedia, New York, Columbia University, Editors, William H. Harris and Judity S. Levey, 1975, 748.

16. Gatz, M., Smyer, M. A., and Lawton, M. P., The mental health system and the older adult, In L. W. Poon, Editor, *Aging in the 1980s*, 1980, 5–18, Washington, DC American Psychological Association.

17. Berger, Bonnie G., Experience, aging, and psychological well-being: The mind-body question, In Andrew C. Ostrow, Editor, *Aging and Motor Behavior*, Indianapolis, Benchmark Press, 1989, 127.

18. Mason, John W., et al, Selectivity of corticosteroids and catecholamine responses to various natural stimuli, *Psychopathology of Human Adaptation*, New York, Plenum, 1976.

19. Cannon, Walter B., *The Wisdom of the Body*, New York, W. W. Norton, 1932.

20. Posner, Israel and Leitner, Lewis A. Eustress vs. distress: Determination by predictability and controllability of the stressor, *Stress, The Official Journal of the International Institute of Stress and Its Affiliates*, Vol. 2, Summer, 1981.

21. Mikhail, Anis, Stress: A psychophysiological connection, *Journal of Human Stress*, June 1981.

22. Holmes, T. H. and Rahe, R. H., The social adjustment rating scale, *Journal of Psychomatic Research*, 11, 1967.

23. Lazarus, Richard S. Little hassles can be hazardous to your health, *Psychology Today*, July 1981.

24. Miller, Mark J. and Wilcox, Charles T., Measuring perceived hassles and uplifts among the elderly, *Journal of Human Behavior and Learning*, 1986, Vol. 3(1), 38–46.

25. Pelletier, Kenneth R., *Mind As Healer, Mind As Slayer*, New York, Dell, 1977.

26. Wolff, Harold G., *Stress and Disease*, Springfield, IL, Charles C Thomas, Publisher, 1968, 2nd ed, Revised and edited by Stewart Wolff and Helen Godell, 1968, 7.

27. Friedman, Meyer, and Rosenman, Ray H., *Type A Behavior Behavior and Your Heart*, New York, Alfred A. Knopf, 1974, ix.

28. Auerbach, Stuart, Doctors say studies fail to prove that stress causes heart attacks, *The Washington Post*, January 22, 1975.

29. Annual meeting of the American Psychiatric Association, Dallas, TX, May 1985.

30. McQuade, Walter and Aikan, Ann, *Stress*, New York, E. P. Dutton, 1974, 7.

31. Frankenhaeuser, Marianne, Women and men said to differ in their response to stress, *Psychiatric News*, June 18, 1975.

32. Humphrey, Joy N., and Everly, George S. Perceived dimensions of stress responsiveness in male and female students, *Health Education*, November/December 1980.

33. Cochran, C. D. and Hale, W. Daniel, Gender differences in the relationship between health and psychological distress in the elderly, *Clinical Gerentologist*, Fall 1984, Vol 3(1), 62–64.

34. Levy, Sandra M., The aging woman: Developmental issues and mental health needs, *Professional Psychology*, February 1981, 92–102.

35. Grant, Peter R., Who experiences the move into a nursing home as stressful?

Examination of the relocation stress hypothesis using archival, time-series data, *Canadian Journal of Aging,* Summer 1985.

36. Rathus, Spencer A. and Nevid, Jeffrey S. *Behavior Therapy,* New York, New American Library, 1977.

37. Whitehead, D'ann, Mariela, Shirley, and Walker, C. Eugene, Use of systematic desensitization in the treatment of children's fears, New York, AMS Press, No. 1 in series on *Stress in Modern Society, Stress in Childhood,* James H. Humphrey, Editor, 1984, 213–215.

38. Watson, J. B. and Tayner R., Conditioned emotional reactions, *Journal of Experimental Psychology,* 1920, 3, 1–14.

39. Mowrer, O. H., A stimulus-response analysis of anxiety and its role as a reinforcing agent, *Psychological Review,* 1939, 46, 553–565.

40. Roberto, Karen A., Stress and adaptation of older osteoporotic women, *Women & Health,* 1988, Vol. 14(3–4) 105–119.

41. Khorana, Suman A., Psychological risk factors in ischemic heart disease, *Indian Journal of Clinical Psychology,* 1989, Vol. 16(1), 13–17.

42. Perri, H. and Templer, D. I., The effects of an aerobic exercise program on psychological variables in older adults, *The International Journal of Aging & Human Development.* 20(3) 167–172, 1984.

43. Cohn, Victor, The disgrace of American health care, *Weekly Journal of Medicine, Science and Society,* January 24, 1989.

44. Palm, J. Daniel, *Diet Away Your Stress, Tension & Anxiety,* New York, Doubleday, 1976.

45. Morse, Donald R. and Pollack, Robert L., *The Stress-Free Anti-Aging Diet,* New York, AMS Press, No. 19 in the series of *Stress in Modern Society,* James H. Humphrey, editor, 1989, 170.

46. *NRTA Bulletin,* February 1991, Vol. 32, No. 2, Washington, DC, 12.

47. Ross, Catherine E., Religion and psychological distress, *Journal of the Scientific Study of Religion,* June 1990, Vol 29(2), 236–245.

48. Ostrow, A. C., Age role stereotyping: Implications for physical activity participation, In Rowles, G., and Ohta, R., *Aging and milieu: Environmental perspectives on growing old,* New York, Academic Press, 1983, 153–170.

49. Conrad, C. C., When you're young at heart, *Aging,* 258, 11–13, 1981.

50. Berger, Bonnie G., and Hecht, Lillian Mushabac, Exercise, aging, and psychological well-being: The Mind-Body Question, In Andrew C. Ostrow, *Aging and Motor Behavior,* Indianapolis, Benchmark Press, 1989, 131–132.

51. President's Council on Physical Fitness and Sports, *Physical Fitness Research Digest,* Series L, July 1971.

52. Berger, Bonnie G., Use of jogging and swimming as stress reduction techniques, In J. H. Humphrey (Ed.), *Human Stress Current Selected Research,* Vol. 1, New York, AMS Press, 1986.

53. McQuade, Walter and Aikman, Ann, *Stress,* New York, E. P. Dutton, 1974, 130.

54. Jencks, Beata, *Your Body Biofeedback at Its Best,* Chicago, Nelson Hall, 1977, 51, 172.

55. Shepard, R. J., Physical activity and aging in a post-industrial society, In B. D.

McPherson, (Ed.) *Sport and Aging,* Champaign, IL, Human Kinetics, 1986, 37–43.

56. Pelletier, Kenneth R. *Longevity: Fulfilling Our Biological Potential,* New York, Dell Publishing, 1981.

57. Trumping father time—but don't toss away your gym shoes, *Modern Maturity,* February/March, 1991, 88.

58. Uson, P. P. and Larrosa, V. R., Physical activities in retirement age, In J. Partington, J. Orlick and J. Samela (Eds.), *Sport in Perspective,* Canada Association of Canada, 1982, 149–151.

59. Bennett, J., Carmadi, M. U. and Gardner, V. I., The effect of a program of physical exercise on depression in older adults, *Physical Educator,* 39, 21–24, 1980.

60. Frekany, G. A., and Leslie, D. K., Effects of an exercise program on selected flexibility measurements of senior citizens, *The Gerentologist* 15(2), 182–183, 1987.

61. Bassett, C., McClamrock, E., and Schmelzer, M., A 10-week exercise program for senior citizens, *Geriatric Nursing,* March/April, 1983, 103–105.

62. Chapman, E. A., de Vries, H. A., and Swezey, R. Joint stiffness: Effects of exercise on young and old men, *Journal of Gerentology* 27(2), 218–221.

63. Perri, H. and Templer, D. I., The effects of an aerobic exercise program on psychological variables in older adults, *The International Journal of Aging and Human Development,* 20(3), 167–172.

64. Bortz, Walter, Inactivity hastens aging: Exercise may slow it down, *Running and Fitness,* January/February, 1983.

65. Pocari, J., et al., Is fast walking an adequate aerobic training stimulus for 30–69-year-old men and women? *The Physician and Sports Medicine,* 1987, 15, 119–129.

66. Gal, Reuven, and Lazarus, Richard S., The role of activity in anticipating and confronting stressful situations, *Journal of Human Stress,* December 1975.

67. Lazarus, Richard S., The self regulation of emotion, In *Parameters of Emotion,* L. Long (Ed.), New York, Raven Press, 1975.

68. Brown, Barbara B., *Stress and the Art of Biofeedback* New York, Bantam, 1978, 31.

69. Benson, Herbert, *The Relaxation Response,* New York, William Morrow, 1975.

70. Yarian, Richard A. Relaxation techniques and the relaxation response, Washington, DC, *AAHPER Research Consortium Papers,* Vol. 1, Book 2, 1978.

71. Steinhaus, Arthur, *Toward and Understanding of Health and Physical Education,* Dubuque, Iowa, Wm. C. Brown, 1963, 73.

72. Jacobson, Edmund, *You Must Relax,* 4th ed., New York, McGraw-Hill, 1962.

73. McBrien, Robert J., Using relaxation methods with first grade boys, *Elementary School Guidance and Counseling,* February 1978.

74. Ardell, Donald B., High Level Wellness, New York, Bantam, 1979, 44.

75. Humphrey, James H., and Humphrey, Joy N., *Reducing Stress in Children Through Creative Relaxation,* Springfield, IL, Charles C Thomas, Publisher, 1981.

76. Woolfolk, Robert L., and Richardson, Frank C., *Stress, Survival & Society,* New York, New American Library, Inc., 1978, 141.

77. Goleman, Daniel J., Meditation helps break the stress spiral, *Psychology Today,* February 1976.

78. Hales, Diane and Hales, Robert, Exercising the psyche, *Health, Weekly Journal of Medicine, Fitness and Psychology,* June 5, 1985.

79. Sethi, Amarjit S., *Meditation as an Intervention in Stress Reactivity,* New York, AMS Press, No. 12 in series on *Stress in Modern Society,* James H. Humphrey, Editor, 1989, 88–101.

80. Bloomfield, Harold H., et al, *TM Discovering Inner Energy and Overcoming Stress,* Boston, G. K. Hall, 1976, 7.

81. Goleman, Daniel J., and Schwartz, G. E., Meditation as an intervention in stress reactivity, *Journal of Consulting and Clinical Psychology,* 44, 1976.

82. Wallace, R. K., Physiological effects of transcendental meditation, *Science,* 167, 1970.

83. Klemons, Ira, M., Change in inflammation in persons practicing transcendental meditation technique, (Pennsylvania State University, University Park, PA), *Scientific Research on the Transcendental Meditation Program: Collected Papers,* Vol. 1, eds., Orme-Johnson, David W. and Farrow, John T., New York, MIU Press, 1975.

84. Shaw, Robert and Kolb, David, One point reaction time involving meditators and non-meditators, (University of Texas, Austin, TX), *Scientific Research on the Transcendental Meditation Program: Collected Papers,* eds., Orme-Johnson, David W., and Farrow, John T., New York, MIU Press, 1975.

85. Kirsch, I. and Henry, D., Self-sensitization and meditation in the reduction of public speaking anxiety, *Journal of Consulting and Clinical Psychology,* 47, 1979.

86. Hall, N. R. and Goldstein, A. L., Think well: The chemical links between emotions and health, *The Sciences,* March/April, 1986, 34–41.

87. Miskiman, Donald E., The effect of the transcendental meditation technique on the organization of thinking and recall, (University of Alberta, Edmonton, Alberta, Canada), *Scientific Research on the Transcendental Meditation Program: Collected Papers,* Vol. 1, eds. Orme-Johnson, David W. and Farrow, John T., New York, MIU Press, 1975.

88. Tojoa, Andre S., Some evidence that the transcendental meditation program increases intelligence as measured by a psychological test, (University of Leiden, Leiden, Holland), *Scientific Research on the Transcendental Meditation Program: Collected Papers,* Vol. 1, eds., Orme-Johnson, David W. and Farrow, John T., New York, MIU Press, 1975.

89. Rosenbaum, Lilian, Biofeedback with family therapy for diabetes mellitus, Vol. 1, *Human Stress: Current Selected Research,* Ed. James H. Humphrey, New York, AMS Press, 1986, 123–132.

90. Rosenbaum, Lilian, *Biofeedback Frontiers,* No. 15 in series on *Stress in Modern Society,* New York, AMS Press, Inc., Ed. James H. Humphrey, 1989, 155.

91. Bilodeau, Edward A. and Bilodeau, Ina, Motor skill learning, *Annual Review of Psychology,* Palo Alto, CA, 1961.

92. Brown, Barbara B., *New Mind New Body,* New York, Bantam, 1975, 5.

93. Stern, Robert M. and Ray, William J., *Biofeedback and the Control of Body Activity,* Homewood, IL, Learning Systems Company, 1975, 1.

94. Brown, Barbara B., *The Biofeedback Syllabus*, Springfield, IL, Charles C Thomas, Publisher, 1975, vi.

95. Culligan, Matthew H. and Sedlacek, Keith, *How to Kill Stress Before it Kills You*, New York, Grossett & Dunlap, 1976, 97.

96. Perkins, Hugh, *Human Development and Learning*, 2nd ed., Belmont, CA, Wadsworth, 1974.

97. Knapp, T. J. and Shodahl, S. A., Ben Franklin as a behavior modifier: A note, *Behavior Therapy*, 5, 1974.

98. Humphrey, James H., *Stress in the Nursing Profession*, Springfield, IL, Charles C Thomas, Publisher, 1988, 68–71.

INDEX